Watercolor by Maribeth Salois

© Copyright 2015
ISBN: 978-0-692-49039-6
To purchase a book contact Wave Walker Bed and Breakfast

Wave Walker Bed and Breakfast
WaveWalkerBedandBreakfast.com
(207) 667-5767

Illustrations
Teddi-Jann Covell
teddi-janncovell.com

Food Photography
Tracy Thurston

Night Sky Photography
Photo of Donna and Phil
Antonio Martin
martinreich.com

Landscape Photography
Sue Michaud
suereflections.net

Book & Cover Design by Monica Wendel
Printed by The Copy Center Plus, Augusta, ME

MAINE
The Way Food Should Be

Favorites from family, friends, and customers of
Wave Walker Bed and Breakfast

Donna Doyen

Theresa + Jay
may the smells coming
from your kitchen remind
you of your stay at Wave
Walker! Donna Doyen

Dedication

I dedicate this book to my grandmother, Irene Gonyea McKinney. She has been an inspiration to me my whole life. She loved to cook, and more importantly, she loved to feed people. She reveled in watching others enjoy the results of her cooking. There were always pots of coffee and black tea on her woodstove. Pie was her specialty. I remember standing on a kitchen chair "stealing" bits of her pie dough or a slice of cinnamon sugared apple. Meanwhile, she was talking to me the whole time - telling me how to make pie crust by counting the cups of flour and showing me how much ice water too add. Her voice is forever imprinted in my memory as she would always detail each ingredient as she added it to the bowl as she made a pie. Her patience was endless.

My grandparents always hosted the family gathering every holiday. There was never a question of where we would go - it was always "the farm." It never occurred to us to go anywhere else. My grandmother cooked every holiday meal until she was well into her 80s. A typical Thanksgiving celebration started Wednesday and the food kept coming until Sunday evening. She would typically cook three turkeys, one ham, potatoes, macaroni salad, vegetables canned from the summer garden, and yes - four to five pies!

Everyone was always welcome at the McKinney farm, and no one ever left hungry. There was no need for a reservation; her door was always open! However, if she knew you were coming you can bet your bottom dollar she would prepare your favorite foods.

This cookbook would not have been possible without my grandmother's endless patience, her passion for cooking great food, and her loving example of hospitality and generosity. These qualities are the cornerstone of Wave Walker Bed and Breakfast and the inspiration for this cookbook.

Contents

Baked Goods...13

Fruit Sensations 41

Breakfast Entrées 51

Appetizers...67

Lobsters and More for Dinner 81

Desserts..97

Donna's Pantry: Sauces, Jams, and Candy...........................121

Acknowledgements 135

About the Author 137

Recipe index..138

Recipe Index Alphabetical...........................141

Key Word Index Alphabetical...........................144

Photo by Antonio Martin

Photo by Antonio Martin

From Farm to B&B

In 1928 Phil's grandmother, Esther Greenstein Kettell, bought an 83 acre farm, which included a 20 acre blueberry field. It was located 8.3 miles down Newbury Neck in Surry, Maine. The farmhouse burned to the ground on July 4, 1968, of an electrical fire. Phil was 10 at the time and lived there with his mother, Elizabeth, and brother, Malcolm.

In 2006 we decided we would build the B&B on a site near the ocean in a corner of the blueberry field. After 3 years of work, in 2010 we completed construction of Wave Walker. In September of that year, we welcomed our first guests.

Photo by Laura Pellerano

Photo by Sue Michaud

Foreword by Linda Greenlaw

MAINE
The Way Food Should Be

Favorites from family, friends, and customers of Wave Walker Bed and Breakfast

Lobster in the front yard - blueberries in the back – and someone who knows what to do with them. Wave Walker B&B is quintessential Maine, and its hosts Donna and Phil Doyen are as warm and welcoming as the blueberry muffins and lobster stew their guests enjoy.

Donna was one of the first people I met when I moved to Newbury Neck, and her love of cooking and entertaining made for an easy friendship. We talk food, comparing recipes while cross-country skiing, in attempt to shed what results from the cooking passion we share. Donna is a natural in the kitchen. Gourmet quality dishes both in taste and presentation are prepared in a gale of Donna's contagious laughter. She loves what she is doing, which is the greatest comfort factor for those lucky enough to experience it.

My first visit to Wave Walker was for breakfast. Wow! The view from every single window is absolutely breath taking. The island-studded Union Bay is a perfect backdrop for any emotion guests are searching to fulfill – relaxing, inspiring, romantic, or just plain fun. The only thing that exceeds the view is the food – a three-course feast, the star of which is a luscious lobster omelet.

I have now seen Wave Walker in every season. And, the beauty of the B&B changes as dramatically as the weather. In the summer, lobster boats circle and haul traps within easy sight from the B&B's front deck where breakfast is served. A dinner invitation on a frigid, snowy night last winter when we ate appetizers in front of a blazing fire resulted in my husband pleading for me to "learn how to cook pork like Donna," an art I have not mastered. Fall is brilliant with the surrounding blueberry bushes a crimson red that compares only to the sunrise over Mount Desert Island. And spring… spring is when the long, cold winter fades in the shadow of Donna's radiance. I proudly recommend Wave Walker to friends, family and business associates. And if I didn't live so close, I would stay there too!

Photo by Sue Michaud

Introduction

Maine, The Way Food Should Be, is a collection of some of the favorite recipes we enjoy at our bed and breakfast, Wave Walker. I have been sharing a variety of recipes with our guests one email at a time since we opened in 2010. Whenever I found an excellent recipe, I would write it in my journal, which I have kept my entire adult life. Unfortunately I do not have all of the recipes documented as to who gave them to me. When known I have given credit to the originator, however on a few of the recipes, I have left the attribution blank when the author is unknown. I apologize in advance for that omission.

My objective is to get folks of all skill levels back in the kitchen. With a spiral binding to lay flat and coated pages, this book should be used, not stored on a shelf. If something spills on it, that's ok - wipe it off and go on! Go ahead and write in it or make yourself little notes in the margin. I do this all the time. Most recipes can be tweaked with your touches or just the word "EX-CELLENT!" to remind you that this was a good recipe and should be made again!

The kitchen is my domain and a gathering place for family, friends, and guests. Whether it's sharing a simple cup of tea with a neighbor, or creating a new taste sensation for future guests, the kitchen is my "happy place." I hope my love of food inspires you to enjoy your kitchen as well. If you have the desire, you too can create great meals! There is no reason to be afraid of the kitchen as so many people are these days. Roll up your sleeves and get right in there. For those who do not have the "desire," please visit us at Wave Walker Bed and Breakfast and leave the cooking to me! As our frequent guests, Judy and Dana Williams boast, "No one spoils them better than Donna does."

Photo by Antonio Martin

Baked Goods

When baking you will need to invest in a set of "dry" and "wet" measuring cups. A dry cup is used for measuring dry ingredients only. Use a scoop to place the ingredients in the measuring cup; do not tap or press down. Take a knife and drag across the top of the cup to level. A wet measuring cup has a spout and is see-thru. To read the level of the liquid being measured, place the cup on the counter and lower your head to read the increments at eye level. It really does make a difference when you use dry and wet measuring cups. Your results will be worth the extra dishes!

Grandma Doyen's Blueberry Muffins
Elizabeth Doyen (Phil's mother)

When we decided to open our B&B, I tried to create my own signature blueberry muffin. I put lemon curd inside, I put a glaze or streusel on top, and nuts, etc. After many different variations my family informed me that they would not try another blueberry muffin unless it was Grandma Doyen's recipe! They said, "You can't improve on the best!"

Cook Time: Convection bake 375º 18 minutes, or bake 400º 21-25 minutes.
Yield: 12 muffins

Ingredients:
1 egg
1/2 cup milk
1/4 cup vegetable oil
1 1/2 cups flour
1/2 cup sugar
1 teaspoon cinnamon
2 teaspoons baking powder
1/2 teaspoon salt
1 1/4 cups blueberries

Directions:
Preheat oven to 400º
or convection bake 375º.
Beat egg, add milk, oil, and sugar.
Stir with fork.
Sift in dry ingredients.
Before stirring add the blueberries and dust them with the dry ingredients
already in the bowl.
Fold in the flour and berries just until all flour is moistened. The batter will still be lumpy.
Be careful not to overstir the batter. Overstirring will result in a tough muffin.
Scoop batter into paper-lined muffin tins.
Bake.

Pumpkin Bread or Muffins
Claire Strong

This recipe was given to me by Claire Strong. She was a neighbor on Green Lake in Ellsworth, Maine. She would make them in 1 pound coffee cans and give them away at Christmas as long as she could keep her husband Charlie from eating all the tops.

Cook Time: Convection bake 300º
1 hour, or bake 350º 1 hour
Yield: 3 loaves or 2 loaves
plus 12 muffins

Ingredients:

3 cups sugar

1 cup oil

4 eggs, beaten

1 (1 lb.) can pumpkin or 2 cups fresh pumpkin

3 1/2 cups flour

1 teaspoon baking powder

2 teaspoons baking soda

2 teaspoons salt

1/2 teaspoon ground cloves

1 teaspoon cinnamon

1 teaspoon nutmeg

1 teaspoon allspice

2/3 cup water

1/2 cup nuts, optional

Directions:
Metal pans: preheat oven to 350º cook 1 hour.
Glass pans: preheat oven to 300º cook 55-65 minutes.
Combine sugar, oil, and eggs. Beat until lemon colored.
Sift together all dry ingredients, add to sugar mixture.
Add pumpkin and water. Fold in nuts.
Spray with Pam or grease and flour 3 loaf pans.
Bake.
When done, cool 10 minutes in pan. Remove from pan and cool on cooling rack.

Muffins:
Instead of making a third loaf of pumpkin bread I sometimes make cranberry walnut muffins.
To do this, I add 1 cup chopped cranberries and 1/2 cup chopped walnuts for a batch of 12 muffins.
Convection bake 375º 18 minutes or bake 400º 21-25 minutes.

Banana Nut Muffins
Donna Doyen

This is a favorite of my husband Phil and daughter Karen. A great way to use up those over-ripe bananas which you can peel and freeze until you are ready to make your muffins.

Cook Time: Convection bake 375º 18 minutes, or bake 400º 21-25 minutes.
Yield: 24

Ingredients:
1 cup sugar
1/2 cup butter, softened
1 egg
2 cups flour
1 teaspoon baking soda
1/2 cup sour cream
1 teaspoon vanilla
4 ripe bananas, mashed with a fork leaving some chunks
1/2 cup walnuts, chopped

Directions:
Preheat oven to 400º, or convection bake 375º.
Beat sugar and butter until light and fluffy, add egg, and vanilla, beat until smooth.
Sift flour and baking soda.
Add flour and baking soda, alternating with sour cream to the sugar mixture.
Stir by hand until just barely incorporated.
Fold in banana and nuts.
Scoop into paper-lined muffin tin.
Bake.

Notes: I use this for a 6 muffin gluten free batch.
Convection bake 375º 18 minutes.
1/4 recipe-6 muffins

1/4 cup sugar	1/2 cup gluten free flour	1/4 tsp vanilla
2 tablespoons butter, softened	1/4 teaspoon baking soda	1 banana
1 tablespoon egg, beaten	2 tablespoons sour cream	2 tablespoons walnuts, chopped

Cranberry Orange Muffins

Cook Time: Convection bake 375º 18 minutes or bake 400º 21-24 minutes
Yield: 12 muffins

Ingredients:
2 cups flour
1 cup cranberries, chopped
2 teaspoons orange zest
1/2 cup orange juice
3/4 cup sugar, divided
1/2 teaspoon salt
2 teaspoons baking powder
2 eggs
1/2 cup oil
1/2 cup walnuts, chopped

Directions:
Preheat oven to convection bake 375º or bake 400º.
Line a 12 muffin tin with paper liners.
Stir cranberries, zest and 1/4 cup sugar, set aside.
In large bowl sift flour, 1/2 cup sugar, salt and baking powder.
Add orange juice, oil and eggs all at once to dry mixture.
Stir just until moist.
Fold in cranberries and nuts.
Scoop into paper-lined muffin tin.
Bake until golden.

Rhubarb, Orange, and Ginger Muffins

Donna Doyen

I love everything rhubarb and these muffins are one of my many favorites. I am like a little kid when I am eating it. I think "this is my favorite," until the next kind of favorite muffin!

Cook Time: Convection bake 375º 16-18 minutes or bake 400º 20-23 minutes
Yield: 24 muffins

Ingredients:
3 cups flour
1 cup brown sugar, firmly packed
2 teaspoons baking powder
1/2 teaspoon baking soda
Zest and juice of 1/2 orange
Plain unsweetened yogurt (see note)*
1 large egg, lightly beaten
1 tablespoon grated fresh ginger root
1/2 cup, (1 stick) unsalted butter, melted
2 cups raw rhubarb, sliced 1/2 inch
(If using frozen rhubarb do not thaw first)

Topping:
1 tablespoon light brown sugar, packed
1 tablespoon sugar
1/2 teaspoon cinnamon
1/2 teaspoon ground ginger spice

Directions:
Preheat oven to convection bake 375º or bake 400º.
Mix dry ingredients and rhubarb in a large bowl.
Place orange zest, orange juice, and yogurt into a one cup measuring cup, to equal 1 cup. See note.*
Pour this into a separate bowl, add egg, fresh ginger, and melted butter.
Stir until combined.
Add wet ingredients to dry ingredients and fold in until the flour is just barely moist. DO NOT OVERMIX.
Scoop mixture into paper-lined muffin tins.
Add topping.
Bake.

Notes:
* Add however much yogurt to the orange zest and juice to equal 1 cup.

 18

Morning Glory Muffins
Donna Doyen

Cook Time: Convection bake 375° 18 minutes or bake 400° 20-23 minutes.
Yield: 24 muffins

Ingredients:
2 cups flour
1 1/4 cups sugar
2 teaspoons baking soda
2 teaspoons cinnamon
1 apple peeled, cored, and diced
1/2 cup raisins (put in pan of boiling water, let set until ready to use, drain, add to mixture)
1/2 cup Baker's Angel Flaked Sweetened Coconut
1/2 cup pecans or walnuts, chopped
2 cups carrot, grated
3 eggs
1/2 cup vegetable oil
1 teaspoon vanilla extract

Directions:
Preheat oven, line muffin tins with muffin papers.
In a large bowl whisk flour, sugar, baking soda, and cinnamon.
Add carrots, apple, raisins, coconut, and nuts. Mix until it resembles a coarse meal.
In a separate bowl beat eggs with a fork, add oil and vanilla mix well.
Pour into the dry ingredients and combine just until all moist. Do not over mix.
Scoop into muffin tins, bake until golden brown.

Notes:
I like to use half golden raisins and half regular raisins. You can also use 1 cup carrot and 1 cup zucchini. You can add just about anything. Use a good quality coconut; the cheaper coconut is dry and will dry out your muffins. I like these muffins because they have everything in them, like a green smoothie in a muffin! I prefer to use my food processor to shred the carrot and zucchini the night before and store it in the refrigerator.

Vegan Carrot Cake Muffins
Laurie Rokakis

Our neighbor, Laurie Rokakis gave me this recipe. Her son Douglas is a vegetarian and she had made these muffins for him. They are very good and I can make them for a crowd and no one would suspect they are vegan. They have so much flavor.

Cook Time: Convection bake 375° 18 minutes or bake 400° 20-23 minutes.
Yield: 24 muffins

Ingredients:
1 cup nondairy milk, almond milk
1 1/2 teaspoons apple cider vinegar
1 3/4 cups whole wheat flour
1/2 cup flour
1 teaspoon baking powder
1 teaspoon baking soda
1 1/2 cups grated carrot (3-4)
3/4 cup chopped or crushed pineapple, drained

3/4 cup raisins, soaked in boiling water, drained
1/2 cup walnuts, chopped
3/4 cup plus 2 tablespoons sugar
1/2 cup oil
2 tablespoons molasses
1 1/2 teaspoons vanilla
1 teaspoon cinnamon
1 teaspoon nutmeg
1 teaspoon salt
1/2 teaspoon cardamom

Directions:
Mix milk and vinegar, set aside.
Preheat oven to convection bake 375° or bake 400°.
Line muffin tins with paper liners.
In a large bowl sift flours, baking powder, baking soda, salt, cinnamon, nutmeg, and cardamom. Set aside.
In another bowl whisk sugar, oil, molasses, and vanilla.
Fold in carrot, pineapple, raisins, walnuts, and milk mixture to the sugar mixture, stir.
Fold wet ingredients into dry ingredients, fold just until moist. Scoop into muffin liners. Bake.

Notes:
I use almond milk which yields a very moist muffin. You wouldn't know they were vegan. You can also substitute craisins for raisins. I like to soak my raisins to plump them, so they don't take the moisture out of your muffins.

Gluten Free Banana Peanut Butter Muffins

According to King Arthur Flour Company this is how to convert traditional recipes to gluten free recipes. This recipe is already converted.
- Substitute the flour for an equal amount of gluten free flour.
- Substitute one large egg for 1/4 cup of the liquid in the recipe, water, oil, or milk.
- Add 1/4 teaspoon of Xanthan gum for each cup of flour.
This works for muffins, quick breads, donuts, and coffee cake but not for yeast breads, or cookies requiring kneading, rising, or creaming butter and sugar together.

Cook Time: Convection bake 375º 17 minutes or bake 400º 20-22 minutes
Yield: 6 muffins

Ingredients:
1/2 cup peanut butter
1 1/2 eggs* see note
1 banana, mashed with a fork
3 tablespoons coconut flour (Gluten free flour)
2 tablespoons sugar
2 tablespoons almond milk
1/4 teaspoon plus 1/8 teaspoon baking soda
1/2 teaspoon vanilla

Directions:
Preheat oven to convection bake 375º or bake 400º.
Line a 6 well muffin tin with paper liners.
Whisk peanut butter, eggs, and banana.
Add the rest of ingredients and fold in.
Fill each cup 3/4 full. Bake.

Note: For 1/2 egg, beat one egg and use half of it, or use 2 tablespoons of Egg Beaters.

Paleo Pumpkin Muffins

Cook Time: 350º 20-25 minutes
Yield: 10 muffins

Ingredients:
1 cup almond flour
1/2 cup coconut flour
1 teaspoon baking soda
1/4 teaspoon salt
3 eggs, lightly beaten
3/4 cup canned pumpkin
3 tablespoons coconut oil, melted
1 teaspoon vanilla
1/4 cup honey
1/4 cup pecans, chopped
1 teaspoon pumpkin pie spice, for topping

Directions:
Preheat oven to 350º.
Whisk almond flour, coconut flour, baking soda, and salt.
In a separate bowl mix eggs, pumpkin, oil, vanilla, and honey.
Add wet ingredients to dry ingredients, stir until just barely combined.
Scoop into muffin liners.
Sprinkle with nuts and pumpkin pie spice.
Bake at 350º 20-25 minutes.

Blueberry Buttermilk Scones
Donna Doyen

While visiting the U.K. in 2014, I had the privilege of watching several bakers make scones. They did not measure and always used buttermilk. Since we live in a blueberry field, I like to use blueberries whenever possible. That is how this recipe came to be. I serve them warm with lemon curd. For special occasions I like to make them heart shaped.

Cook Time: 400º 15 minutes
Yield: 16

Ingredients:
3 cups flour
1/3 cup sugar
1 teaspoon salt
2 1/2 teaspoons baking soda
3/4 cup unsalted butter
1 cup buttermilk
1 1/2 cups blueberries
1 tablespoon heavy cream, for brushing

Directions:
Preheat oven to 400º.
Whisk dry ingredients, cut in butter, fold in berries, add buttermilk, and stir just until moistened.
Divide dough in half.
Pat down on floured surface to a 3/4 inch thick round circle.
Cut into 8 pie shaped pieces.
Put on a cookie sheet lined with parchment.
Brush scones with heavy cream.
Bake at 400º 15 minutes.

Note: Lemon curd recipe is on page 122.

Buttermilk substitution: 2 tablespoons lemon juice plus enough milk to equal 1 cup.

Blueberry Almond Scones with Lemon Curd

Donna Doyen

Cook Time: 375º for 20-25 minutes

Scone ingredients:
2 cups flour
1/2 teaspoon salt
1/4 cup sugar
2 1/2 teaspoons baking powder
6 tablespoons cold butter
1 cup blueberries
2 eggs, beaten
1/2 cup vanilla yogurt

1 teaspoon vanilla
1 tablespoon lemon zest
1/2 teaspoon almond extract
2 tablespoons coarse sugar (for top) optional
1/4 cup sliced almonds (for top) optional

Lemon curd:
4 egg yolks
3/4 cup sugar
3 ounces freshly squeezed lemon juice
4 tablespoons butter, melted
Pinch of salt
2 teaspoons lemon zest

Directions:
Preheat oven to 375º.
Grease scone pan with butter.
Whisk dry ingredients together.
Add butter with fingers until crumbly, or cut in with a pastry cutter.
Add blueberries.
In a separate bowl, mix eggs, yogurt, vanilla, lemon zest, and almond extract.
Add to dry ingredients.
Stir gently until just combined (moist).
Place on scone pan, and level out the dough. Sprinkle with coarse sugar and sliced almonds.
Bake at 375º for 20-24 minutes.

LEMON CURD:
In saucepan, beat yolks and sugar with whisk until well blended.
Stir in lemon juice, butter and salt.
Cook over medium heat, stirring continuously, until it coats the back of a metal spoon.
Strain with a mesh strainer then add lemon zest.

Notes: Reheat at 350º, loosely wrapped in foil, for 8-10 minutes.

Gluten Free Blueberry Coconut Scones

I discovered this recipe when searching recipes for Dick, a gluten free guest. The first time I made him scones they came out as chewy patties. He said I could call them blueberry patties and keep the recipe because he liked the taste. On his second visit I experimented on him and his wife again. This time it was a home run.

Cook Time: 350º 35-40 minutes
Yield: 9 inch round cake pan, serves 6

Ingredients:
1 egg
1/4 cup coconut oil, melted
1/4 cup sugar
1 1/2 cups almond flour
2 teaspoons arrowroot powder or cornstarch
1 teaspoon vanilla
3/4 cup blueberries
1/4 cup Baker's Angel Flaked Sweetened coconut
1 teaspoon baking powder
1 teaspoon coarse sugar, optional

Directions:
Preheat oven to 350º.
Line 9 inch round cake pan with parchment paper up the sides.
Beat egg, coconut oil, and sugar.
Add rest of ingredients except blueberries and mix.
Fold in blueberries.
Bake at 350º 35-40 minutes.
Cool in the pan 15 minutes.

Rhubarb Coffee Cake
with Caramel Sauce

I love rhubarb. This coffee cake is amazing with or without the sauce, but with the sauce it's over the top! I have to make this when I have a houseful or else I will eat it until it is gone. Rhubarb and daffodils are the two best things about spring in Maine.

Cook Time: 350º 35-40 minutes
Yield: 9X13 pan

Cake Ingredients:
1/2 cup Crisco
1 1/2 cups sugar
1 egg
2 cups flour
1 teaspoon baking soda
1 cup buttermilk
3 cups chopped rhubarb, fresh or frozen, not thawed

Topping:
1/4 cup flour
1/2 cup brown sugar, packed
1 teaspoon cinnamon
3 tablespoons butter, cold

Caramel sauce:
1 cup brown sugar, packed
1/2 cup half and half
4 tablespoons butter
Pinch salt
1 tablespoon vanilla

Directions:
Preheat oven to 350º.
Grease and flour a 9X13 pan.
In a large bowl beat Crisco and sugar until light and fluffy.
Add egg, beat well. In a separate bowl combine flour and baking soda,
add to creamed mixture alternating with buttermilk.
Fold in rhubarb. Pour into baking pan.
In a small bowl combine brown sugar, flour and cinnamon.
Cut in butter, sprinkle over batter.
Bake at 350º 35-40 minutes until cake tester comes out clean.

Meanwhile in a heavy saucepan, mix brown sugar, half and half, butter and salt, whisk.
Over medium heat whisk constantly 5-7 minutes, add vanilla cook 1 minute longer.
Cool. Serve over individual pieces of coffee cake.
Store any leftover sauce in the refrigerator.

Rhubarb Coffeecake

Cook Time: 350º 45 minutes

Yield: 1 Bundt cake

Cake ingredients:
1 1/2 cups brown sugar, packed
2/3 cup vegetable oil or melted butter
1 egg
1 teaspoon vanilla
2 1/2 cups flour
1 teaspoon salt
1 teaspoon baking soda
1 cup milk
2 cups rhubarb, sliced 1/2 inch
1/2 cup slivered almonds

Topping:
1/2 cup sugar
1 tablespoon butter, cold
1/4 cup slivered almonds

Glaze: Optional
3/4 cup confectioners sugar
2-3 ~~tablespoons~~ whole milk
teaspoons

Directions:
Preheat oven to 350º.
Grease and flour a Bundt pan.
In a large bowl beat together brown sugar, oil or butter, egg, and vanilla.
In a separate bowl sift together flour, salt, and baking soda. Stir dry ingredients into the batter alternating with milk. Beat until smooth.
Fold in the rhubarb and almonds.
Pour batter into Bundt pan.

Topping:
Cut butter into sugar, add almonds.
Sprinkle over cake.
Bake at 350º for 45 minutes until cake tester comes out clean.
Cool in pan 10 minutes, then invert onto a cooling rack.

Glaze:
Whisk confectioners sugar and milk. Glaze the side without the nuts while still warm.

Rhubarb Coffeecake with Streusel & Glaze

Cook Time: 350º 45 minutes

Yield: 9X13 OR 2-9X9's

Cake ingredients:
1 cup sugar
1/2 cup butter
1 egg
1 cup buttermilk
2 cups flour
1 teaspoon baking soda
1 teaspoon cinnamon
3 cups rhubarb, sliced 1/2 inch

Streusel topping:
1/2 cup sugar
3/4 cup walnuts, chopped
1 teaspoon cinnamon
1 tablespoon butter, melted

Glaze: Optional
2/3 cup confectioners sugar
2-3 ~~tablespoons~~ *teaspoons* whole milk

Directions:
Preheat oven to 350º.
Grease and flour pan.

Cake:
Cream sugar and butter, beat in egg and buttermilk.
In another bowl sift flour, baking soda, and cinnamon, then add to sugar mixture.
Mix together, fold in rhubarb. Spread in pan.
Mix topping and sprinkle on top of cake batter.
Bake at 350º 45 minutes until cake tester comes out clean.
Whisk confectioners sugar and milk to drizzle on top of warm cake!

Poppy Seed Cake
Betty Beardsley

Betty gave me this for Christmas this past year! WOW it's so good. It doesn't even need the glaze. It's a good thing this recipe makes two loaves or I would never give one away. When I made it, I didn't have butter flavoring so I just used the same amount of butter.

Cook Time: 325º 1 hour
Yield: 2 loaves

Ingredients
3 cups flour
2 1/2 cups sugar
1 1/2 teaspoons salt
1 1/2 teaspoons baking powder
3 eggs
1 1/2 cups milk
1 cup plus 2 tablespoons oil
2 tablespoons poppy seeds
1 1/2 teaspoons vanilla extract
1 1/2 teaspoons almond extract
1 1/2 teaspoons butter flavored extract

Glaze:
1/4 cup orange juice
3/4 cup sugar
1/2 teaspoon vanilla extract
1/2 teaspoon almond extract
1 1/2 teaspoons butter

Directions:
Preheat oven to 325º.
Mix all cake ingredients together until smooth.
Grease and flour two bread pans.
Pour batter in the two pans.
Bake 1 hour, until cake tester comes out clean.

Prepare glaze:
In a heavy saucepan bring all ingredients to a boil. Brush glaze on warm cakes with a silicon brush.

Cinnamon Streusel Coffeecake
Avis Black

Avis is Phil's cousin from Veazie, Maine. She made this recipe for church brunches. It is so easy yet tastes amazing. The hardest part of this recipe is remembering to add the sour cream before pouring the batter into the pan.

Cook Time: 350º 35 to 40 minutes
Yield: 9X13

Ingredients:
2 boxes Pillsbury Cinnamon Streusel Bread mix for 9X13 pan
   (1 box Pillsbury Cinnamon Streusel Bread mix for 9X9 pan plus 1/4 cup sour cream
   and half of the topping)
Ingredients to make the cake per box directions plus 1/2 cup sour cream

Topping:
1 cup walnuts, chopped, optional
2/3 cup brown sugar, packed
2 tablespoons butter, melted
1 1/2 teaspoons cinnamon

Directions:
Preheat oven to 350º.
In a small bowl combine all topping ingredients and set aside.
Make cake according to directions, then fold in sour cream.
Spread half the batter into a greased and floured 9X13 pan. Sprinkle all of the streusel mix from the box on top of the batter.
Carefully spread the remainder of batter on top.
Sprinkle with homemade topping.
Bake at 350º 35 to 40 minutes until toothpick comes out mostly clean.
Cool slightly, drizzle glaze on top.

Notes:
During apple season I add peeled, cored and chopped apple chunks.

Blueberry Cream Cheese Coffeecake

Cook Time: 350º 1 hour
Yield: 10-12

Ingredients:
2 cups flour
1 teaspoon salt
2 teaspoons baking powder
1 cup sugar
2 teaspoons cinnamon
1 cup walnuts, roughly chopped
2 eggs
1/2 cup vegetable oil

Cream cheese layer:
8 ounces cream cheese, softened
1/3 cup sugar
1 egg
Pinch of salt
1 teaspoon vanilla

Fruit topping:
2 cups blueberries
1/3 cup sugar
1 tablespoon lemon juice
Zest of 1 lemon
1/3 cup water
1 tablespoon corn starch

Directions:
Preheat oven to 350º.
Grease and flour a 9X13 baking pan.
Sift dry ingredients in a large bowl, add nuts.
In a small bowl beat eggs and oil,
add to dry ingredients, stir until combined.
Press into baking pan.
Combine all ingredients from the cream cheese layer, spread over the crust.
In a saucepan combine blueberries, sugar, lemon juice, and zest.
Mix cornstarch and water until dissolved, add to the saucepan, and bring to a boil, stirring constantly over medium heat.
Pour over cream cheese mixture and spread out.
Bake one hour, cool on a rack.

   31

Apple Pound Cake

Donna Doyen

I created this recipe when we lived in Merrimack, NH. We lived next to Currier's Orchard, a family run apple orchard. For two seasons we made the pies, cakes, and pumpkin bread for the Curriers to sell at their orchard.

Cook Time: 375º 1 hour
Yield: 1 Bundt cake

Ingredients:
1 1/2 cups oil
2 cups sugar
3 eggs
1 teaspoon vanilla
1 teaspoon salt
1 teaspoon baking soda
1 teaspoon cinnamon
3 cups flour
3 cups apples, peeled and cut in chunks
1 cup nuts, optional

Directions:
Preheat oven to 375º. Grease and flour Bundt pan or two loaf pans.
Cream oil and sugar.
Add eggs one at a time, beat until lemon colored.
Sift dry ingredients together.
Remove 1/2 cup of the flour mixture and toss with the apples.
Add flour mixture to sugar mixture 1 cup at a time.
Mix with hand mixer.
Fold in apples by hand. It will look like a lot of apples.
Pour into prepared Bundt pan.
Bake at 375º for 1 hour.

Done when toothpick comes out clean.
Serve with ice cream.

Blood Orange Yogurt Bread

This is beautiful and sweet. The blood orange gives this bread a nice pink color.

Cook Time: 350º 50-60 minutes
Yield: 1 loaf

Ingredients:
1 cup flour
2 teaspoons baking powder
1/2 teaspoon salt
1 cup plain, whole milk, Greek yogurt
1 cup sugar
3 eggs
Zest 2 blood oranges
1/2 teaspoon vanilla
1/2 cup vegetable oil

Topping:
1 tablespoon sugar
1/3 cup fresh blood orange juice

Glaze:
1 1/2 -2 tablespoons blood orange juice
1 cup confectioners sugar

Directions:
Preheat oven to 350º, grease and flour glass bread pan.
Sift flour, baking powder, and salt.
In another bowl whisk yogurt, 1 cup sugar, eggs, vanilla, zest, and oil.
In a large bowl fold dry ingredients into wet ingredients a little at a time, stir just until moist.
Pour into bread pan.
Bake at 350º 50-60 minutes until a cake tester comes out clean.

In a small saucepan combine and heat 1/3 cup blood orange juice and 1 tablespoon sugar until sugar dissolves and it is clear.
Set aside.
Cool cake 10 minutes in the pan, then turn out onto a cooling rack.
Pour orange juice mixture onto cake, let absorb, cool completely.

Glaze:
Whisk blood orange juice and confectioners sugar, glaze cooled cake.

Notes:
You can substitute grapefruit or lemons for blood oranges.
It's very pretty with the blood orange!

Zucchini Bread
Irene McKinney

This is my grandmother's recipe. She didn't write many down but I have a few. She liked to throw in different ingredients like pineapple or apples into her sweet breads. She would keep this in the refrigerator. I am not sure if it was to hide it from my grandfather or make it last longer.

Cook Time: 350º 50 minutes
Yield: 2 loaves

Ingredients:
4 eggs
2 cups sugar
1 cup vegetable oil
2 cups unpeeled zucchini, shredded*
3 1/2 cups flour
3/4 teaspoon baking powder
1 1/2 teaspoons baking soda
1 teaspoon salt
1 teaspoon cinnamon
1 1/2 teaspoons vanilla
1 cup walnuts, coarsely chopped
1 cup raisins, soaked in boiling water, drained

Directions:
Preheat oven to 350º.
Beat eggs and sugar. Add oil.
Sift dry ingredients and add to sugar mixture, alternating with zucchini.
Add remaining ingredients.
Mix.
Pour into 2 greased and floured loaf pans.
Bake for 50 minutes.
Cool in pan for 10 minutes.
Remove from pan onto a cooling rack.

* If it is a large zucchini, scoop out and discard the seeds.

Irish Brown Bread

I got this recipe from a museum in Ireland when we visited our daughter Katherine while she was studying abroad in Wales. It is so easy and good. This bread does not need time to rise, just mix and bake. We stayed in B&B's throughout the UK. In Ireland they served this with our breakfast, toasted with jam. That was the first time I saw an English toast rack.

Cook Time: 400º 40 + 15 minutes
Yield: 1 loaf

Ingredients:
3 1/2 cups white flour
2/3 cup whole wheat flour
1 cup plus 1 tablespoon oat bran
1/4 cup sugar
1 teaspoon baking soda
1 teaspoon cream of tartar
1/2 egg (2 tablespoons), beat egg then measure out 2 tablespoons.
1 1/2 cups buttermilk

Directions:
Preheat oven to 400º.
Mix all ingredients in a large bowl.
Grease and flour your loaf pan.
Put batter in pan.
Bake at 400º for 40 minutes turn off oven, leave bread in the oven for 15 more minutes.
Remove from oven.
Cool 10 minutes in the pan then remove to a cooling rack.

Pecan Sticky Buns Yeast Dough

Dough will need to set overnight, then plan 2 hours 45 minutes in the morning to rise and bake.

Cook Time: 350º 20 -30 minutes, internal temperature 185º-188º
Yield: 12 Rolls 9 X 13 baking dish

Dough ingredients:
1/2 cup milk
1/2 cup water, 110 degrees
2 1/4 teaspoons yeast, 1 packet
1 1/2 teaspoons salt
2 teaspoons vanilla
8 tablespoons unsalted butter
1/2 cup sugar
1 egg plus 2 egg yolks
4-4 1/4 cups flour

Caramel sauce:
2 cups sugar
1 cup water
1 teaspoon vanilla
2 tablespoons corn syrup
3/4 cup heavy cream
4 tablespoons unsalted butter
A pinch of salt
2 cups coarsely chopped pecans, toasted in a 350 degree oven 10 minutes, divided 1/2 cup & 1 1/2 cups.

Filling:
4 tablespoons butter, softened
3/4 cup light brown sugar, packed
1/4 teaspoon salt
3/4 teaspoon nutmeg
1 teaspoon cinnamon
1/2 cup pecans

Directions:

Dough: melt butter, add milk, heat to 100 degrees.

In stand mixer with paddle, mix water, yeast, sugar, vanilla, egg and yolk on low until mixed.

Add salt, warm milk mixture, and 2 cups flour.

Mix on medium speed 1 minute, until well blended.

Switch to dough hook, add 2 cups flour, and mix on #2 setting 10 minutes until dough pulls away from sides of bowl. You can add 1/4 cup flour if needed.

Place in lightly greased bowl, cover with towel, place in 100° oven 1 1/2-2hours.

While dough rises make caramel sauce.

Caramel sauce:

Combine sugar and water in a 2 quart saucepan.

Cover and bring to a boil over high heat.

Once boiling, uncover.

When syrup is thick and straw colored about 7 minutes or more, temperature on a candy thermometer should be 300° at this point.

Reduce heat to medium, continue to cook until syrup is golden and begins to smoke 1-2 minutes. The temperature should now be 350°.

Meanwhile bring cream, butter, vanilla, salt, and corn syrup to a simmer over high heat in a small saucepan.

If cream mixture reaches a simmer before caramel sauce reaches 350°, remove from heat and set aside.

As soon as syrup reaches 350°, remove from heat and pour about 1/4 of the cream mixture into it, let the bubbles subside.

Add remainder of cream, whisk until smooth. While hot, pour into baking dish, sprinkle with 1 1/2 cups roasted pecans, set aside.

After dough has doubled in size, punch down. Put dough on lightly floured surface.

With rolling pin roll to a 16x12 rectangle with the long side facing you left to right.

Combine filling ingredients plus 1/2 cup nuts in a small bowl.

Spread filling over dough leaving a 1/2 inch border at the edge.

Roll up dough rolling up the long edge so the roll will be 16 inches long.

Cut into 12 pieces, placing cut side up in baking dish. Cut dough in half, then cut each half in half again. Then cut into thirds.

Refrigerate overnight or let rise 1 1/2 to 2 hours. If in refrigerator overnight, take out and let rise 2 hours in a 100° degree oven.

Bake in middle rack 25-35 minutes at 350° until internal temperature reaches 185° to 188°.

Cool in pan 5 minutes, invert on a large platter.

With rubber spatula scrape out the caramel and spread over top of buns.

Cool 10 minutes, serve warm.

Blueberry Yeast Rolls
Donna Doyen

Four words is all you will need to describe this recipe; light, fluffy, lemony, heaven!

Cook Time: 350° 35-40 minutes
Yield: 15

Ingredients:
2 (1/4 ounce) packages active dry yeast or 4 1/2 teaspoons
1/4 cup warm water 110°
1 1/2 cups buttermilk
1/2 cup vegetable oil
4 1/2 cups flour
1 teaspoon salt
1/2 teaspoon baking soda
2 cups frozen blueberries
1/2 cup melted butter
Juice of 1 lemon (3 tablespoons)
1/2 cup sugar
Zest of 1 lemon
GLAZE:
1 cup confectioners sugar
4-6 teaspoons lemon juice

Directions:

In a measuring cup, dissolve yeast in warm water- 110 degrees.

Let stand until creamy, about 10 minutes.

Heat buttermilk in the microwave 30 seconds twice until warm to the touch.

In stand mixer, combine buttermilk, oil, and yeast. Mix well with a dough hook.

In a smaller bowl, whisk flour, salt, and baking soda.

Stir flour mixture into liquid 1 cup at a time until a soft dough forms on setting #1 or 2.*

Knead with dough hook 5-8 minutes, on setting #2.*

Turn dough out onto lightly floured surface and knead by hand 8-10 times.

Cover and rest 15 minutes.

In a small bowl, stir melted butter and lemon juice.

On a well-floured surface roll dough out into a large rectangle 15X22 inches.

Spread lemon butter mixture over dough.

Sprinkle with 1/2 cup sugar.

Spread blueberries over the dough, leaving 1 inch at the top bare for sealing the seam later.

Roll into a log starting on the long edge. The finished roll will be 22 inches long.

Slice into 1 1/2 inch pieces. Place cut side up into a lightly greased 11X15 baking pan.

Cover and let rise 30 minutes or cover and refrigerate overnight.

I refrigerate overnight then take it out and let it come to room temperature 1 hour before baking.

Preheat oven, bake at 350º 30-35 minutes until golden brown.

GLAZE:

Whisk together 1 cup powdered sugar and 4-6 teaspoons lemon juice.

Pour over hot rolls.

Let rest 2-3 minutes before serving.

Note:* Setting numbers refer to a Kitchenaid stand mixer.

Fruit Sensations

When I buy spinach and kale, I freeze it immediately in plastic sandwich bags. In the morning I add one bag of frozen kale or spinach, fruit and or yogurt to the Vitamix and blend until creamy and smooth. I don't usually use a recipe; I just use the ripe fruit I have on hand. However when using greens and blueberries, the color will be brown. Although it now looks like mud, it tastes great!

If buying a Vitamix I recommend going to their website and getting a refurbished model. The refurbished models are considerably less expensive than the new models.

Spinach Grape Pineapple Smoothie
Donna Doyen

Ingredients:
1/2 cup green grapes
1 peeled and seeded orange
4-5 strips orange peel
1 banana
1/2 cup pineapple
1 cup spinach or 1/2 cup spinach and 1/2 cup kale
1 kiwi, peeled
1 1/2 cups ice cubes
1/2 cup water

Directions:
Process all ingredients in a Vitamix or other high-speed blender.
Blend until smooth.
Serve immediately.

....

Tropical Smoothie
Donna Doyen

Ingredients:
1 cup plain Greek yogurt
1 cup mango
1/2 cup pineapple
4-5 strawberries

1 banana frozen
3 tablespoons coconut milk or:
    1 teaspoon coconut oil, melted and
    3 tablespoons milk.

Directions:
Process all ingredients in a Vitamix or other high-speed blender.
Blend until smooth.
Serve immediately.

Blueberry Smoothie

Donna Doyen

Ingredients:
1/2 cup frozen blueberries
1/2 cup milk
1 banana
2 tablespoons raw cashews or cashew butter

Directions:
Process all ingredients in a Vitamix or other high-speed blender.
Blend until smooth.
Serve immediately.

....

Peanut Butter Banana Chocolate Smoothie

Donna Doyen

Yield: 3 cups

Ingredients:
1 cup unsweetened almond milk
1/2 cup vanilla low-fat Greek yogurt
1 tablespoon ground flaxseed
1 tablespoon unsweetened cocoa powder
3 tablespoons creamy peanut butter
1/2 teaspoon vanilla
2 frozen bananas

Directions:
Process all ingredients in a Vitamix or other high-speed blender.
Blend until smooth.
Serve immediately

Kale Apple Lemon Smoothie

Donna Doyen

This smoothie is my personal favorite!

Ingredients:
1 cup kale
1 cup spinach
2 cups green grapes
1 peeled and seeded orange
4-5 strips orange peel
1/2 peeled and seeded lemon
4-5 strips lemon peel
1/2 peeled cucumber
1/2 cored green apple
1 cup mango
2 cups ice
1/2 cup water

Directions:
Process all ingredients in a Vitamix or other high-speed blender.
Blend until smooth.
Serve immediately.

Baked Pears

Cook Time: 350º 30 minutes
Yield: 4

This is a recipe you can easily make at home which will have your family and friends raving.

Ingredients:
2 ripe pears, Bartlett or D'Anjou, peeled, halved, and cored.
Cinnamon
Nutmeg
2 tablespoons melted butter
2 tablespoons brown sugar
Vanilla yogurt * see note
Mint leaf for garnish

Directions:
Preheat oven to 350º.
Peel pears, cut in half
lengthwise and core.
Place pears cut side down
in a pie plate.
In a microwave safe bowl melt butter,
add brown sugar, and stir.
Sprinkle pears with a dusting of cinnamon and a light dusting of nutmeg.
Spoon butter/sugar mixture over the pears.
Bake at 350º 30 minutes.
Serve hot over a bed of vanilla yogurt.
Garnish with a mint leaf.

Notes:
Use Bartlett or D'Anjou pears; Packham pears stay too firm. I prefer Dannon Light vanilla yogurt as it is very creamy.

Baked Pears with Fresh Ginger and Honey

Donna Doyen

Cook Time: Bake 350º 30 minutes
Yield: 4

Ingredients:
2 pears, Bartlett or D'Anjou, peeled, halved, and cored
1 teaspoon fresh ginger, grated
2 tablespoons butter
2 tablespoons honey
Vanilla yogurt
Handful cranberries, for garnish
Mint leaf, for garnish

Directions:
Preheat oven to 350º.
Peel pears, cut in half lengthwise and core.
Place in pie plate flat side down.
I use 1/2 pear per person.
In a small bowl melt butter, add ginger and honey stir, drizzle over pears.
Add a handful of fresh or frozen cranberries for color.
Bake at 350º for 30 minutes.

Notes:
Serve over vanilla yogurt with a sprig of mint. I prefer Dannon light vanilla yogurt because it is very creamy. One time I used Packham pears and they did not get soft and creamy. I had to cut them into bite-size pieces and serve over yogurt. Hence I do not recommend Packham pears.

Poached Plums
Richard Johnson

Richard is a neighbor of ours and is known for his gourmet multi-course dinners. He is from Scotland and this is a favorite of his. He serves the poached plum with a splash of heavy cream. Here at Wave Walker we serve it as a fruit course with Dannon light vanilla yogurt.

Cook Time: 30 minutes
Yield: As many as you want

Ingredients:
Plums
Zest of a lemon
1/4 cup light brown sugar
Dannon vanilla yogurt or heavy cream
Mint leaf, for garnish

Directions:
Bring a pan 3/4 full of water to a boil, add plums, lemon zest, and brown sugar. Reduce heat once it boils again to a simmer. Simmer 30 to 40 minutes. The plums are done when you stick a fork in them and they are soft.

Notes:
Serve over vanilla yogurt or with a splash of heavy cream. Garnish with a sprig of mint.

Poached Peaches with Grand Marnier Reduction

Donna Doyen

Inspired by Charlie Miller. After serving Charlie and his wife Heidi poached plum and baked pear, he asked if I made a poached peach. The peaches were flown in by our cousin Bruce from NJ and were so sweet. This is the result of that conversation. This is definitely a new hit at Wave Walker!

Cook Time: 35 minutes
Yield: as many as you want

Ingredients:
2/3 cup sugar
1/2 cup orange juice
2 cups water
Zest of an orange in long strips
1 vanilla bean
Peaches
1 ounce Grand Marnier
Low fat Dannon yogurt, vanilla
Mint leaf, for garnish

Directions:
In a saucepan bring water, sugar, orange juice, zest, and vanilla bean to a boil.
Turn down to simmer, add the peaches.
Simmer 8 minutes covered, turn the peaches over, cover and simmer 8 more minutes.
Remove from pan and let cool a bit.
Skin the peaches and cover with Saran Wrap, set aside to cool to room temperature.
Remove the vanilla bean, cut in half lengthwise and scrape out the seeds and add both the bean and seeds, back into the pot.
Boil the water mixture on medium-high heat, until it reduces to 1 cup, about 10 to 15 minutes.
Strain into a measuring cup, add 1 ounce of Grand Marnier.
Cut the peach in half and remove the pit.
Serve on top of Dannon yogurt.
Drizzle a couple spoons full of the reduction on top of the peach.
Garnish with a mint leaf.

 48

Soft Custard

Irene McKinney

I like to top this with half a banana and a handful of berries. My mother used to call me and say she wasn't feeling quite right and could I make her a soft custard. I would make a double batch and she would feel better in a flash.

Cook Time: 25 minutes total
Yield: 4 servings

Ingredients:
1 1/2 cups milk
4 egg yolks or 2 whole eggs
1/4 cup sugar
1/4 teaspoon salt
1 teaspoon vanilla
Fruit like banana or berries to eat with it, optional

Directions:
In a double boiler scald the milk.
In a bowl beat the egg, sugar, and salt.
Add 1 cup hot milk to the egg mixture, mix well then pour back into the double boiler.
Stir constantly until it coats the back of a silver spoon.
Cool quickly in a large bowl of ice water.
Add vanilla.
Store in the refrigerator.

Peach Torte

Donna Polinski

This recipe was given to me by Patrick Guthrie, who had received it from Donna. Patrick had given me this recipe at least three times, since I misplaced it so often. I am glad I have such patient friends as I can be somewhat disorganized with all the recipes I want to make! Isn't that what "junk" draws are for? When I contacted Donna to get permission to use this recipe she said it originally came from West Germany when she was stationed there in the U.S. Air Force.

Cook Time: 450º for 10 minutes then reduce to 400º, bake an additional 25 minutes then cool 20 minutes.
Yield: 8 servings

Ingredients:
Crust:
1/4 cup butter, softened
1/3 cup sugar
1/4 teaspoon vanilla
3/4 cup flour
2/3 cup pecans, finely chopped

Filling:
8 ounces cream cheese, softened
1/4 cup sugar
1 egg, room temperature
1/2 teaspoon vanilla

Topping:
1 teaspoon sugar
1 teaspoon cinnamon
2-15 ounce cans of peaches, sliced

Crust directions:
In a food processor with the metal blade, chop pecans, then add butter, sugar, vanilla, and flour.
Pulse until all incorporated.
Press mixture in the bottom and sides of a tart pan or 11 inch springform pan.
Preheat oven to 450º.

Filling directions:
Either in the food processor or with a hand mixer (depending how soft your cream cheese is, if you forgot to take it out of the refrigerator early enough, use the food processor with the metal blade), mix all filling ingredients, just until blended.
Pour over crust.

Topping directions:
In a small bowl mix the cinnamon and sugar. Add drained peaches, stir.
Arrange in a pinwheel pattern starting at the outside of the pan working in.
Bake 10 minutes at 450º, reduce heat to 400º and bake an additional 25 minutes.
Cool at least 20 minutes before removing from the pan.

Breakfast Entrées

Photo by Sue Michaud

Lobster Omelet

Donna Doyen

This recipe came about because my husband Phil fished five lobster traps one summer. Even though it was only five traps, we had more lobster than we could eat ourselves. Lobster is much better fresh; I really don't like to freeze it. When our guests see me cleaning lobster, they know they are in for a special treat the next morning. I usually make lobster omelets once a week in the summer.

When we serve lobster omelets, it comes with "The Wave Walker Challenge"; since you started the day with lobster, to complete the challenge you must eat lobster for lunch and dinner the same day! Many of our guests have successfully completed "The Challenge." Some have even exceeded it by having lobster 4 times in the same day!

Yield: 2 omelets

Ingredients:

1/2 cup lobster, cut to bite size pieces, plus 2 claws for garnish

1/8 teaspoon lobster roe, optional

2 tablespoons butter

1/2 cup heavy cream

2 teaspoons scallions, sliced

Tabasco sauce to taste

6 eggs

Pinch salt

2 teaspoons water

Freshly grated cheddar cheese

Directions:

In a large frying pan, melt butter and a little roe if you have some.

Add lobster and scallions. When meat is hot, add cream and turn down to low. Add a few drops of Tabasco sauce, then move to the back burner on low heat.

For each omelet, whisk:

3 eggs, 1 teaspoon scallions, a couple drops Tabasco sauce, pinch of salt, and 1 teaspoon of water. Over medium heat in a 10 inch frying pan, add butter to the bottom and sides of the skillet. And add egg mixture. When cooked on one side, flip over and cook the other side.

Slide your eggs onto a plate and add 1/4 cup lobster meat and cream to the omelet.

Fold the omelet in half. Place lobster claw on top, grate some cheddar cheese and garnish with hot cream sauce around plate.

Notes: You can also make this with two eggs and the same amount of lobster-cream mixture. Use 1/4 cup lobster plus a claw per omelet. When preparing lobster to be cooked later, be careful not to overcook. Boil water, add the lobster, when the water returns to a boil, cook 6 minutes. (I always use sea water to cook the lobster). Salt your water well, 1/4 cup, if not using sea water. Clean and put aside the meat in the refrigerator until the morning.

Crustless Mini Crab Quiche
Donna Doyen

This recipe is a customer favorite. I think our guests like to eat local fare and the Maine crabs are excellent. In the winter I substitute Maine shrimp for the crab. As an option I can scoop out some of the quiche mixture and add bacon or leave just cheese for those who do not like crab.

Cook Time: Bake 350º for 20-22 minutes
Yield: 18 Mini Crab Quiches

Ingredients:
Cooking spray
2 cups cheddar cheese, shredded
3/4 cup half and half
3/4 cup reduced fat Hellman's mayonnaise
4 eggs
3 tablespoons flour
1/2 teaspoon Lawry's seasoned salt
1/8 teaspoon pepper
1/4 cup finely sliced green onions, scallions
1/2 pound crab meat

Directions:
Preheat oven to 350º.
Combine cheese, half and half, mayonnaise, eggs, flour, seasoned salt, pepper, and scallions in bowl, whisk. Fold in crab.
Spray muffin pan with non-stick cooking spray.
Fill each muffin cup 3/4 full with quiche mixture.
Bake at 350º for 20-22 minutes.
The quiche will puff and then deflate.
Garnish with green onion, chives, or a nasturtium flower.

Note: When I have gluten free guests, I leave out the flour and the quiche is still delicious.

German Apple Pancake

My mother loves her baked apple pancake. When she went to her favorite restaurant for German Apple Pancakes, she found it had closed. She called me very disappointed and said she would miss those pancakes. As a surprise when she visited me, I made this for her breakfast. She loved it and so do our guests.

Cook Time: preheat to 500º
            reduce to 425º bake 16 minutes
Yield: 3 servings

Ingredients:
2 large eggs
3/4 cup half and half
1 teaspoon vanilla
1/2 teaspoon salt
1 tablespoon sugar
1/2 cup flour
1 tablespoon butter
3 Granny Smith apples peeled,
    cored, and sliced
1/4 cup light brown sugar
Maple syrup, warmed

Directions:
Preheat oven to 500º. Reduce to 425º when you put the pancakes in the oven.
Mix eggs, half and half, vanilla, salt, flour, and granulated sugar in a bowl, whisk. Set aside.
In a 10 inch nonstick skillet melt butter on medium-high heat, when foamy add apples and brown sugar.
Cook, stirring often for 5 minutes, then 3 to 4 more minutes stirring constantly until the syrup is thick and bubbly and the apples have softened but still hold their shape.
Remove from heat.
Whisk batter and pour on top of apples, around the edge first then to the middle.
Reduce heat to 425º place in oven, bake 16 minutes.
Remove from oven.
Flip over onto a plate and serve hot with real maple syrup.

Note:
I learned the hard way, after removing the pancake from the oven, I now leave a potholder on the pan handle to remind me it is still hot!

Raspberry Stuffed French Toast
Donna Doyen

I wanted a signature French toast dish, and after much experimentation I finally got it right. This recipe is one of our guest favorites. Most recipes I had seen had jam, instead of fresh raspberries. When I substituted fresh raspberries in lieu of the jam, I knew I had a hit. During blueberry season I spread a thin layer of blueberry jam on top of the cream cheese side, then put blueberries in the middle. I have also used strawberries but raspberries are my personal favorite.

Cook Time: Convection bake 375º 10 minutes or bake 350º 15 minutes
Yield: 6

Ingredients:
8 ounces cream cheese
Challah bread, 1 loaf makes 6 servings
Fresh raspberries, 2 pints
2 eggs
1/2 cup half and half
2 tablespoons sugar
1/4 teaspoon vanilla
Dash of salt
Maple syrup served warm
Butter to taste

Directions:
Pre-heat oven to 375º convection bake or bake 350º.
Convection bake 375º for 10 minutes, no need to flip
Or regular bake 350º for 15 minutes, flipping after 10 minutes.
Slice bread into thin slices.
Spread a thin layer of cream cheese on one side of every slice of bread.
In a shallow dish whisk eggs with the salt, half and half, sugar, and vanilla. Whisk until smooth.
Dip the opposite side of bread into the egg mixture, (the side without the cream cheese).
Put egg side down on a cookie sheet lined with parchment paper.
Place raspberries onto cream cheese side, dip the non-cream cheese side of the remaining bread and place the cream cheese side on top of the raspberries.
The cream cheese sides will be together against the raspberries and egg dipped sides on the outside.
Bake.
Serve with real maple syrup and butter.

Lemon Raspberry French Toast Strata

Terence Janericco

Terrance holds a cooking class at his home in Brooklin, Maine, weekly during the summer. One year my cousin Megan and I attended several of his classes. During each class Terrance cooks 4-6 recipes; we watch and learn then enjoy the creations on his porch overlooking the beautiful waters of Herrick Bay. I thought his strata was delicious and I now make it for our guests to enjoy.

Cook Time: 350º 50-55 minutes, cool 5 minutes
Yield: 9 X 13 pan

Ingredients:
1/2 cup real maple syrup, plus additional for serving.
6 cups country-style white bread with crusts, cut in 1 inch cubes.
2 cups fresh raspberries
6 large eggs
4 cups whole milk
1 teaspoon lemon zest
1/4 teaspoon salt

Directions:
Preheat oven to 350º.
Lightly butter a 9X13 baking dish.
Pour 1/2 cup maple syrup in the baking dish, add bread and raspberries.
In a large bowl whisk eggs, milk, lemon zest, and salt; pour over bread cubes.
Bake strata until puffed and golden brown, about 50-55 minutes. Let cool 5 minutes.
Serve warm with additional maple syrup.

Notes:
You can make this recipe ahead and cover and store in the refrigerator overnight. Bring to room temperature in the morning for 45 minutes, then bake as directed.

Egg Crêpes
Donna Doyen

Inspired by: Customer suggestion
A customer, I can't remember who, said a favorite of his while growing up in Maine was to scramble an egg and put blueberry jam in the middle. I was hesitant at first but I kept thinking about it and one day decided I just had to give it a try. Surrounded by a blueberry field, I really enjoy recipes which make use of all those wonderful berries just outside our door. Wow, it was delicious!

Cook Time: 2 minutes

Ingredients:
Cooking spray
Egg, scrambled
Blueberry jam

Directions:
Whisk an egg, heat an 8 inch skillet, and spray with cooking spray.
Pour egg into pan, swirl pan to create a thin egg layer over the entire bottom of the pan.
Cook about 1 minute then flip.
Cook additional 30 seconds to 1 minute then slide out onto a plate.
Top with warm blueberry jam or sauce.
Roll up and serve hot.

Crème Brulee French Toast

Make the night before

Cook Time: 350º 35-40 minutes
Yield: 9X13 baking dish

Ingredients:

1 cup light brown sugar, packed
1/2 cup unsalted butter, melted
2 tablespoons corn syrup
5 eggs plus 2 egg yolks or 6 eggs
1 3/4 cups half and half
3 tablespoons Grand Marnier or orange juice
2 teaspoons vanilla
1/8 teaspoon salt
1 loaf challah bread or French bread,
    cut into 1 inch slices

Berry sauce:
2 cups raspberries
2 cups strawberries
1/3 cup sugar
1/2 cup orange juice
2-3 tablespoons lemon juice

Directions:
In a small saucepan whisk brown sugar, butter, and corn syrup. Bring to a boil.
Pour into a large rimmed baking dish.
Spread sugar mixture into an even layer using a spatula.
Layer the bread on top of the sugar mixture.
In a bowl mix eggs, half and half, Grand Marnier, vanilla, and salt. Whisk and pour over the bread. Cover with foil and refrigerate overnight.
In the morning preheat oven to 350º.
Bake 35-40 minutes. Leave foil on for the first 15 minutes.

Prepare berry sauce:
Combine all ingredients in a Vitamix or high-speed blender.
Place processed ingredients in a saucepan and heat over medium heat until warm.
Serve with French toast.

Breakfast Sausage Strata

Donna Doyen

Cook Time: 1 hour total. Make the preceding night.
Yield: 8-10

Ingredients:
1 1/2 pounds Jimmy Dean sausage (tube)
6 slices white bread, crust removed
1 1/2 cups freshly grated cheddar cheese
8 eggs
2 cups half and half
1 teaspoon salt
1 teaspoon dry mustard
1 teaspoon basil
1/8 teaspoon pepper
1 small onion, minced, sautéed lightly

Directions:
Lightly butter a 9X13 baking pan.
Brown sausage, stirring until it is crumbled.
Drain on paper towels.
Remove crust from bread, cut into 1 inch cubes.
Spread bread around in pan, top with sausage.
Spread cheese over sausage.
In a bowl combine the remaining ingredients and beat well. Pour over casserole.
Cover and refrigerate overnight.
In the morning, warm the casserole to room temperature, about 45 minutes.
Bake at 350º 30 minutes.
Remove from the oven, cut into squares and serve hot.

Notes:
To make for two or three people cut the recipe in thirds, use three eggs and put it in a metal bread pan.

Aebleskivers

This is a traditional Scandinavian recipe for stuffed pancakes. Our cousin's son JB calls this dish "little balls of goodness," and is delighted when I make them for him. You will need a special Aebleskiver pan, which you can get on the internet. It has 7 cups for the batter molded into the pan. I use a nonstick pan by Nordic Ware.

Cook Time: 4 minutes
Yield: serves 4

Ingredients:
1 1/2 cups flour
2 teaspoons baking powder
1/2 teaspoon salt
3 eggs
1 cup milk
3 tablespoons butter, melted

Filling: Banana, raspberries, Nutella, peanut butter, cooked sausage, any other filling you choose.
Maple syrup.

Directions:
In a bowl whisk flour, baking powder, and salt.
Add eggs, milk, and butter. Whisk until smooth.
Heat pan on low heat.
Prepare filling ingredients:
Cook sausage in patties, then cut into 1 inch pieces. Slice banana or whatever you want in the middle of your pancake. Have everything cut up and ready near your pan.
Turn the heat up to medium, the pan is ready when a drop of water sizzles when dropped into a well of the pan.
With a silicone brush lightly butter the wells. Working quickly put half of a small scoop of batter in each well.
Place filling in the middle, top the filling with another 1/2 scoop of batter. The batter should now be even with or slightly above the top of the well. Cook about 2 minutes.
Using a small rubber spatula push down on one side of the Aebleskiver until it rotates 180 degrees, making a ball. Cook 2 minutes more until golden brown.
It will be golden brown like a pancake. Serve hot with warm maple syrup, jam, confectioners sugar, and/or butter.

Notes:
We like to experiment with the fillings. I usually serve a sausage round then a dessert round. We have even used 1/4 of a peanut butter cup! Yum! Sometimes guests come up with one like banana, chocolate and peanut butter.

Corned Beef Hash

Kelly Sawyer

MarKel's Bakehouse, Castine, Maine

I met Kelly Sawyer at a Chinese cooking class in Bucksport. While there we exchanged a few favorite recipes. Our daughter Beth enjoyed going to MarKel's while attending Maine Maritime Academy for their scrumptious baked goods.

Cook Time: 225º overnight
Yield: 10-12 servings

Ingredients:
Corned beef brisket
Orange juice
Water
Several tablespoons pickling spice,
    normally it comes in the brisket package

4 bay leaves
2 tablespoons peppercorns
2 onions
Red potatoes
Nutmeg
Salt and pepper to taste

Directions:
Brown beef on both sides in a skillet.
Pour equal amounts orange juice and water to cover beef in a deep roasting pan or crockpot.
Add several tablespoons pickling spice, 4 bay leaves, 2 tablespoons peppercorns, and an onion, cut in half.
Cover and bake at 225º overnight or 8 hours until meat breaks apart with a fork, or in a or in a crockpot on low, 8 hours.
When meat is cool enough to handle, remove all the fat and discard.
Shred the meat while still warm.
Parboil red potatoes until still firm.
Cut potatoes into cubes between 1/4 and 1/2 inch square.
Chop onion and sauté until soft.
Add potatoes to onion, cook until potatoes start to brown and get slightly crispy. Add salt and pepper.
Add a little nutmeg, optional.
Add corned beef and sauté 5 minutes, until meat is heated throughout.
Serve with a poached egg on top.

Stuffed Portobello Mushroom Delight

Donna Doyen

This recipe came about from an appetizer that I make called Mushroom BLT. I was eating eggs, spinach, salsa, and feta for breakfast just after I typed the Mushroom BLT recipe on my I Pad for this cookbook, and the light came on. This recipe was born.

Cook Time: 350º 30 minutes

Ingredients:
Large Portobello mushroom caps
Spinach, steamed
Eggs, scrambled, 2 per mushroom cap
Salsa, medium hot – optional
Feta cheese, or goat cheese, crumbled
Bacon, cooked crisp, crumbled
2 tablespoons olive oil
2 tablespoons balsamic vinegar
Tomato, diced, for garnish on top

Directions:
Preheat oven to 350º.
Whisk olive oil and balsamic vinegar.
Wipe mushrooms with a wet paper towel. Remove stems and gills.
Brush both sides of the mushrooms with the oil and vinegar.
Line a baking dish with foil. Place mushrooms gill side down, bake 5 minutes.
Turn mushrooms over, bake 5-10 minutes more. Remove from oven and set aside.
Meanwhile, fry bacon crisp, crumble. Steam spinach, drain water.

Assemble your breakfast.
Place each mushroom cap on a plate, add spinach, salsa, cheese, scrambled eggs, bacon, and top with diced tomato.
Serve immediately.

Zucchini Frittata

Yield: 8-10

Ingredients:
6 medium sized zucchini
2 cloves garlic, pressed
1/3 cup olive oil
20 eggs
3/4 cup milk
1 tablespoon salt
1 teaspoon freshly ground pepper
1/2 cup fresh sweet basil, chopped
1/2 cup Parmesan cheese
Paprika, garnish, optional
10 fresh basil leaves, garnish

Directions:
Preheat oven to broil.
Slice zucchini into 1/2 inch slices then chop coarsely.
In a 12 inch skillet heat 2 tablespoons olive oil, add zucchini and garlic, sauté until almost soft.
Remove from pan and set aside.
In a large bowl beat the eggs, milk, salt, pepper, and basil.
Add remainder of oil to the pan, when heated, add egg mixture to the pan.
Cook until almost done add zucchini back into the pan, cook until semi firm, top with cheese, paprika, and basil.
Place under the broiler a few minutes, until slightly browned.
Slice into wedges, top each slice with a fresh basil leaf, serve immediately.

Notes:
This is a great way to use some zucchini. I also add mushrooms and spinach sometimes.

Apple, Sage, and Fennel Sausage
Terence Janericco

Yield: 16 patties

Ingredients:
1 tablespoon oil
2 tart apples (Granny Smith), peeled, cored and, 1/4" dice
1 bunch scallions, thinly sliced
2 pounds ground pork
1/2 cup fresh sage leaves, minced
1 1/2 teaspoons fennel seeds, crushed
1 teaspoon salt
3/4 teaspoon pepper

Directions:
Heat pan and oil.
Add apples and the white part of the scallions.
Cook just until it begins to brown.
Cool 10 minutes in a bowl.
Crush the fennel with the flat side of a large knife on a cutting board.
Mix all ingredients together including cooled apple and onions.
Make into patties (3 inches by 3/4 inch). Should make 16 patties.
Cook in a frying pan until done.

Parmesan Potatoes

Whenever we serve this dish we get rave reviews.
This side dish is crunchy and very tasty.

Cook Time: 350º 1 hour to 1 1/2 hours
Yield: 4 servings

Ingredients:
6 medium potatoes
1/2 cup grated Parmesan cheese
1/4 cup flour
1 teaspoon salt
1/2 teaspoon pepper
4 tablespoons butter

Directions:
Melt the butter in a 350º degree oven
on a cookie sheet or baking stoneware pan with sides.
Peel potatoes and cut up into bite size chunks.
In a large bowl toss potatoes, Parmesan cheese, flour, salt, and pepper.
Place potatoes on the baking pan on top of the melted butter.
Bake 30 minutes, flip potatoes, and bake 30 minutes more.
Leave in the oven until you are ready for them.
They can cook another half hour depending on how crisp you like them.

This is a great breakfast potato. Excellent when served with an egg dish.

Appetizers

Clockwise from top: Scallops Wrapped in Bacon, Caprese Roasted Tomatos, Beef Tenderloin with Horseradish Cream, Easy Crab Dip on Bread, Beef Tenderloin with Horseradish Cream, Portobello Mushroom wih Bacon and Tomato.

Maine Lobster Stew
Donna Doyen

This was first served when I hosted a dinner party for Dennis and Margaret Rackliffe of Rackliffe Pottery in Blue Hill, Maine. It really made an impression and their daughter Suzy thought this recipe should be included in the book. This one is for you, Suzy!

Cook Time: 2 days. 1 hour 30 minutes prep
Yield: 4

Ingredients:
4 lobsters, at least one female for the roe
4-6 tablespoons butter
2 cups heavy cream
2 cups whole milk
Salt and pepper, to taste
(I used white pepper so you don't see it)
Generous 1/2 cup good sherry
Oyster crackers

Directions:
Bring a large pot of sea water or salted water to a boil. Put the lobster in and when water returns to a boil, boil 4 to 6 minutes and remove the lobster. When cool enough, clean.
Clean the lobster, save the tomalley and roe.
Put the tomalley, (green) and roe, (red) in a blender with a little of the milk and blend until smooth.
In a heavy pot, add butter and lobster meat. Sauté until warm, 4-5 minutes. When the butter turns red add sherry.
Add cream, milk, and tomalley and roe mixture, simmer for 15 minutes DO NOT BOIL.
Let cool and refrigerate overnight. (If you have time the flavors will be enhanced).
Warm up and serve the next day.
Clean out lobster heads and discard the contents.
Trim the back part of the head with scissors to the desired size and place them in boiling water to clean. Boil for 5 minutes.
Remove from water and store with 16 lobster legs in the refrigerator until ready to serve.
When ready to serve bring a small pan of water to a boil.
Heat the legs and heads in the boiling water, so it doesn't cool down your stew.
When ready to serve the stew, heat it slowly, but do not boil.
Serve in bowls with the head and legs as a garnish.

Notes:
If you don't have heavy cream, you can use 4 cups half and half.

Easy Crab Dip on Bread

Donna Doyen

This recipe is a hit at any cocktail party. It is still very good even at room temperature. If I am in a real rush, I skip browning the bread and it is still excellent.

Cook Time: broil, 1-2 minutes
Yield: Platter full

Ingredients:
1 loaf bread, French or Italian
1 10 ounce block of cheddar cheese, shredded

Mayonnaise
1/2 pound crab meat

Directions:
Preheat broiler.
Mix crab meat and cheese, add enough mayonnaise for it to hold together.
Slice bread 1/2 - 3/4 inch thick and lay out on a cookie sheet. Broil until lightly browned.
I leave the door open and watch because I have burned too many! Spread the crab mixture on the soft side of the bread and put back under the broiler for a 1-2 minutes until bubbly.

....

Crab Dip

Bonnie Torrey and Jean Messex

Bonnie held a "Business after Hours" event for the chamber of commerce in Blue Hill, Maine. No one strayed very far from this dip! She was so gracious to share this recipe.

Cook Time: 350º 45-50 minutes. Make 12-24 hours ahead

Ingredients:
1/2 pound crab meat
2 tablespoons finely chopped mild onion, cooked until clear

1/2 cup mayonnaise
1 egg, beaten
Garlic salt to taste
8 ounces softened cream cheese

Directions:
Beat cream cheese, egg, garlic salt, and mayonnaise. Fold in crab and onion.
Fill baking container half full.
Cover and refrigerate 12-24 hours.
Bake at 350º for 40-45 minutes in a 9x9 pan.

Scallops Wrapped in Bacon
Donna Doyen

This recipe is quick and easy. If you are expecting guests, get the scallops ready for the broiler and set aside. Pop them into the oven or grill when you are ready.

Cook Time: 15

Ingredients:
1 pound dry sea scallops
1 pound bacon, half cooked

Directions:
Cook the bacon until slightly crispy but still pliable.
Drain on paper towels. Set aside.
Remove the little rubbery piece on the side of the scallop if present and discard.
Wrap the scallop with a slice of bacon, secure it with a wooden toothpick.
Place the scallops on a cookie sheet and broil for 2 minutes.
Remove from oven.
Flip scallops over and broil for one to two minutes more.
Or you can cook them on a grill for 2-3 minutes per side depending how hot your grill is.
Be careful not to overcook.

Caprese Roasted Tomatoes
Megan McCollum

"Oh my God" is what people say as they stuff their faces with this appetizer. Plan a light dinner because they will fill up on these.

Cook Time: 2- 2 1/2 hours
Yield: 15

Ingredients:

15 Campari or cocktail tomatoes, hulled, and drained
1/4 cup plus 1 tablespoon olive oil
2 tablespoons plus 1 1/2 teaspoons balsamic vinegar
4 large garlic cloves
2 teaspoons sugar
Salt and pepper to taste
Fresh basil, big bunch
Baguette
Fresh Mozzarella cheese, sliced

Directions:
Preheat oven to 275º
Cut the tops off of the tomatoes, using a grapefruit spoon or strawberry huller, clean out seeds and ribs of the tomato leaving the shell and tomato attached to it. Put upside down on a paper towel to drain.
Press garlic into a dish and set aside.
Slice some basil into thin ribbons. (7 leaves)
Arrange tomatoes hole side up on parchment paper on a rimmed cookie sheet.
Put a pinch of garlic and a pinch of chopped basil into each tomato.
Sprinkle the sugar over all the tomatoes.
In a measuring cup whisk the oil and vinegar and drizzle in the tomatoes.
Grind some salt and pepper over the tomatoes.
Bake at 275º, check after an hour. They should be compressed down and starting to brown.
Using tongs, pour the liquid inside of the tomatoes out and reserve.
Return to the oven. Check after each 15 minutes until done. They are done when still pliable and compressed. Let cool.
Slice baguette, brush with olive oil. Bake at 350º until just starting to very lightly brown.
Remove from oven. Peel a garlic clove and rub on each toast.
Layer toast, slice of Mozzarella cheese, a basil leaf and a tomato.
In a measuring cup pour the reserved liquid from the cookie sheet and 1 tablespoon of olive oil, and 1 1/2 teaspoons of balsamic vinegar.
Whisk and drizzle over the platter of hors d'oeuvres.
You may have some leftover juice.

Beef Tenderloin with Horseradish Cream

Sherry Fletcher

This appetizer is a favorite at The Surry Garden Club. We host the annual Christmas party for the garden club here at Wave Walker Bed and Breakfast and this appetizer is always a hit.

Ingredients:
Beef tenderloin roast
French bread
1/2 cup heavy cream
1/2 teaspoon salt
Few grains cayenne pepper
2 tablespoons prepared horseradish
1 tablespoon plus 1 teaspoon balsamic vinegar

Directions:
Peel any silver skin from the tenderloin, cook to rare or medium rare. Can be done a day ahead of time.
Cool, slice beef very thin.
Cut French bread thin, 1/4 inch slices.

Make horseradish cream:
In a bowl beat heavy cream until stiff, fold in salt, horseradish, balsamic vinegar, and cayenne pepper.

Assemble:
Layer bread, roast beef, horseradish cream. Enjoy!

Portobello Mushrooms with Bacon and Tomato
Donna Doyen

This recipe came about because I have a neighbor Steve who is gluten sensitive. Steve loves my baked stuffed mushrooms but I wanted to do something different, so I was thinking BLT with a mushroom. I love balsamic vinegar and knew the lettuce wouldn't hold up so I substituted basil.

I have also created a breakfast dish from this idea called "Stuffed Portobello Mushroom Delight", served on a bed of wilted spinach with an egg topper.

Cook Time: 350° 15 minutes
Yield: 1 dozen

Ingredients:
Portobello mushrooms, appetizer size (medium), stems removed, and chopped
1/2 red onion, chopped fine
1/2 cup goat cheese, crumbled
Tomato, diced and tossed in 1 tablespoon oil and balsamic vinegar
6 slices bacon, cooked crispy, crumbled
1/4 cup olive oil
1/4 cup balsamic vinegar
Salt & pepper
1 tablespoon fresh basil, chopped

Directions:
Preheat oven to 350°
Line baking dish with foil.
Whisk oil and vinegar together.
Place 1 tablespoon oil and vinegar in a skillet, heat, add onions and chopped mushroom stems. Cook until onions are translucent.
Toss tomatoes with 1 tablespoon oil and vinegar.
Brush both sides of the mushrooms with the remainder of oil and vinegar.
Place mushrooms in baking dish gill side down.
Bake 5 minutes, flip over and bake 3 - 5 minutes more depending on the size of the mushrooms. Remove from the oven.
Place onion mixture in the cap, add cheese, and bacon. Top with chopped tomato, salt, pepper and basil.

Baked Stuffed Mushrooms

Donna Doyen

Cook Time: 350º 15-20 minutes
Yield: 24

Ingredients:
24 mushrooms 1 1/2-2 inches
1/4 cup chopped green onion
2 tablespoons dry white wine
1/2 cup chopped deli ham or cooked sweet sausage
1/4 cup bread crumbs, can use gluten free
1 tablespoon butter
2 teaspoons flour
1/4 teaspoon basil
1/8 teaspoon pepper
2 tablespoons Parmesan cheese
Top with a piece of Swiss cheese

Directions:
Wipe mushrooms with damp towel, remove stems.
Chop stems and onion, sauté in butter until tender.
Add flour, basil, 1/8 teaspoon pepper, wine, and 2 tablespoons water. Cook until thick and bubbly, add ham, bread crumbs, and Parmesan cheese.
Fill caps, top with Swiss cheese.
Bake at 350º 15-20 minutes until tender.

Notes:
These always disappear and can easily be made gluten free by using gluten free bread crumbs and flour.

Arugula and Beet Salad
Tracy Thurston

Cook Time: 1 hour 15 minutes
Yield: 6 servings

Ingredients:
1/4 pound small beets, trimmed and scrubbed
5 ounces arugula
4 ounces goat cheese, crumbled
1/4 cup candied walnuts,
   (1/4 cup sugar, 1 cup walnuts, and salt)
Avocado peeled and pitted, cut into bite sized pieces

Dressing:
1/2 shallot, minced
1 tablespoon freshly squeezed lemon juice
3 tablespoons freshly squeezed orange juice
1 teaspoon orange zest
1/2 teaspoon Dijon mustard
2 tablespoons extra virgin olive oil
Kosher salt and freshly ground pepper

Directions:
Preheat oven to 400º.
Wrap beets in foil and place on a cookie sheet. Bake 45 minutes to 1 hour until a knife easily slides through the beets. Cool, use a paper towel to peel the beets. Cut into bite size pieces.
Candied walnuts:
Turn oven temperature down to 325º.
Spread nuts on a rimmed baking sheet. Bake stirring occasionally until golden, about 3 minutes. Remove from oven, cool on the pan. In a saucepan over medium-low heat add 1/4 cup sugar, stir until melted and light caramel colored. Remove from heat, add walnuts, stirring to coat. Spread walnuts onto the baking pan working quickly, separate the walnuts to create an even layer. Lightly sprinkle with salt. Set aside to cool. Store in an air tight container.
In a small bowl whisk together the dressing ingredients.
Assemble the salad with arugula, beets, and avocado. Drizzle with dressing and top with goat cheese and candied walnuts.

Notes:
Make the beets and candied walnuts ahead of time. Store in air tight containers until ready to use. I make a big batch of beets and store them in the refrigerator with some balsamic vinegar and olive oil drizzled over them and use them in salads all week.

Blueberry Crostinis

Cook Time: 425º 20 minutes
Yield: plateful

Ingredients:
Goat cheese
Basil
2 garlic cloves
1 cup blueberries
1/2 cup pecans, coarsely chopped
2 tablespoons maple syrup
Baguette sliced thin
Olive oil

Directions:
Preheat oven to 425º.
Slice baguette, brush with olive oil and sprinkle with chopped garlic.
Place on a cookie sheet.
Bake at 425º for 8 minutes.
Put blueberries on cookie sheet.
Bake at 400º for 6 minutes.
Chop up 10 basil leaves and a chunk of goat cheese, mix together and spread on bread.
Top with blueberries.
In frying pan mix pecans and maple syrup and bring to a boil.
Pour over blueberries serve.

Black Bean Dip, Fat Free
Sherry Fletcher

A group of ladies from Surry play cards on Wednesday afternoons. Someone is always trying to lose weight, usually me. This dip is tasty with an assortment of fresh vegetables.

Ingredients:
2 - 15 ounce cans black beans, drained, reserve liquid
3-4 cloves garlic, pressed
2 teaspoons salt
1 tablespoon balsamic vinegar
2 teaspoons chili powder, can add more to taste
1/2 jalapeño pepper, seeded and chopped
1 teaspoon lemon zest
2 tablespoons lemon juice

Directions:
Mix all ingredients together in food processor.
Add bean liquid until desired consistency is reached. I prefer this dip when it is thick.

Baked Beans with Ham and Bacon
Betty Mathien

I got this recipe from Brenda Schofield years ago. I have lost it several times and I contacted Brenda in a panic for it once again. My girls and I love this recipe; other recipes just don't compare! This recipe came from Brenda's aunts' mother-in-law, Betty Mathien. She has since passed away but her recipe lives on! I love old family recipes.

Cook Time: 5 hours plus soak overnight
Yield: 9X13 pan

Ingredients:
1 pound dry beans (great northern or yellow eye)
Leftover ham with bone or ham steak
1 large onion, chopped
1 cup brown sugar
3/4 teaspoon dry mustard
1 teaspoon pepper
2 tablespoons ketchup
1 tablespoon molasses
Bacon slices to cover casserole
1 teaspoon salt, optional *see note

Directions:
Soak beans overnight.
In the morning, drain and rinse beans, add ham bone and onion.
Add water to cover beans by three inches. Bring to a boil then reduce heat to medium.
Cook until tender, 1 1/2 to 2 hours.
Remove ham bone, when cool enough cut off all the meat and add it back to the beans.
Add the rest of ingredients to the beans including the liquid the beans were cooked in.
Mix well and pour into casserole dish or bean pots.
Cover with bacon slices.
Bake at 300º-325º for 3 hours or until brown and bacon is cooked.

Notes:
I usually double the recipe with one ham bone with a lot of meat left on it. It makes a great gift and freezes well. I leave the salt out because I think it is salty enough with the ham and bacon.

Black Bean Soup

John Baumgarten

Owner and chef of Caribbean Chicken, a restaurant in Palmetto, FL., a gluten-free haven.

This recipe has been adapted from John's Uncle Robert Baumgarten. Robert has been a chef for 46 years. Originally he trained in France. He later trained cruise ship chefs. When John showed interest in opening a restaurant that he could specialize in gluten free fare, his uncle sent him a large envelope of recipes and advised him to jot down changes so he could repeat his success later. John has a big heart and is always helping those less fortunate.

Cook Time: 2 1/2 days
Yield: 8-10

Ingredients:
2 cups black beans
1 cup garbanzo beans
1 cup pinto beans
1 tablespoon sazon spice
1 tablespoon adobo spice
1/2 tablespoon chicken base
2 bay leaves
1 pound ham or ham bone with meat

1 pound hot chorizo sausage, skin removed and discarded
1 pound bacon, cut to 1 inch pieces
2-3 celery stalks including leaves, sliced
2-3 carrots, cut in half lengthwise then into chunks
1 Vidalia onion, diced
3 potatoes, peeled and cubed
1 teaspoon bijol

Directions:
Put dry beans in a large stock pot.
Cover beans with at least 4 inches of water above the beans. Refrigerate overnight.
In the morning drain and rinse well.
Put beans back in the pot, fill the pot with water 2-3 inches above the beans.
Add sazon, adobo, bay leaves, and chicken base*.
Cook on low heat, stirring often, for 6-8 hours.
Cool and refrigerate overnight.
The next day, heat beans.
In a large skillet fry up bacon until it starts to crisp up then add ham and chorizo.
Add to soup, grease and all. Add the cut up vegetables and bijol, simmer around 2 hours until vegetables are soft.

*Chicken base is a paste-like chicken flavor similar to bullion. If not in your grocery store it can usually be found in health food or specialty stores or online.

Lobsters and More for Dinner

New England Lobster Pie
Mary Cahoon

I was buying lobster from a fisherman many years ago and I struck up a conversation with his wife Mary. I asked her what her favorite lobster recipe was and she said it was lobster pie. I asked her if she shared her recipes and she handed me a copy that she had already printed up! My favorite way to serve this is over a big crispy baked potato. It could also be served over toast points, rice, noodles, you get the idea.

Cook Time: 30 minutes, plus additional time to cook lobster
Yield: 4 servings

Ingredients:
10 tablespoons butter, divided
1/2 cup good quality sherry
2 cups lobster meat, cut into bite size pieces
2 tablespoons flour
1 1/2 cups half and half
4 egg yolks, beaten

Topping:
1/2 cup Ritz Crackers, crushed
1/2 teaspoon paprika
2 tablespoons Parmesan cheese
4 tablespoons butter, melted

Directions:
Melt 4 tablespoons butter, add sherry, and boil 1 minute.
Add lobster and remove from heat.
In medium saucepan melt 6 tablespoons butter, add flour, and cook until mixture bubbles.
Remove from heat. Set aside.
Drain and reserve the sherry from the lobster meat.
Slowly stir the reserved sherry and the half and half into the butter-flour mixture, stirring until completely blended.
Return to heat stirring constantly until sauce is smooth and thick.
Spoon 4 tablespoons of sauce into a small bowl, add beaten egg yolks 1 tablespoon at a time. Stir well after each addition.
Return egg mixture to the sauce, mix well. Stir over low heat about three minutes.
DO NOT ALLOW TO BOIL!
Remove from heat, add lobster. Turn into 4 individual ramekins or small deep dish pie plate.
Combine topping ingredients and sprinkle over pie.
Bake about 10 minutes until heated through.

Lobster Macaroni and Cheese

Terence Janericco

This is a rich and creamy dish. I like to make this on the rare occasion I have leftover lobster that isn't spoken for.

Cook Time: Bake 375º 30 minutes
Yield: 8-10

Ingredients:
Salt and pepper to taste
12 ounces macaroni
4 tablespoons butter
1/4 cup flour
4 cups milk
11 ounces fontina cheese, grated and divided
8 ounces mascarpone cheese
3 tablespoons lobster broth, clam juice or fish broth
3 tablespoons cognac
1 teaspoon Tabasco sauce
1/2 pound barely cooked lobster meat in 1/2 inch chunks
2 scallions, thinly sliced and divided
2 ounces white cheddar cheese, grated

Directions:
Preheat oven to 375º.
Boil salted water, add macaroni cook 3-5 minutes until half cooked drain, and set aside.
In a large saucepan melt butter, add flour, whisk until foamy. Whisk in milk, one third at a time.
Cook until sauce is thickened and smooth.
Remove from heat, stir in 2 cups fontina, mascarpone, clam juice, cognac, Tabasco, salt and pepper.
Stir in macaroni, 3/4 of the lobster, and scallions.
Turn into a 9X13 pan then sprinkle with remaining fontina and cheddar.
Bake until golden, about 30 minutes, cool 10 minutes.
Garnish with remaining lobster and scallions.

Scallops with Pumpkin Cream Sauce
Maria Messier

Scallop season in Maine is in the winter. When my husband and I were younger, we spent several scallop seasons scuba diving for them. That said, I want my scallops fresh! I like to buy two to three gallons of scallops right off the boat! I take them home and enjoy a scallop dish with these fresh from the ocean treats. I then freeze the remainder in Ziploc freezer bags. They won't last long! Bacon and scallops just go together! Yum, that sounds like a recipe for another omelet!

Cook Time: 25 minutes
Yield: 3-4 servings

Ingredients:
1 pound dry sea scallops
2 tablespoons butter
1 cup canned pumpkin
1/2 cup heavy cream
1/2 pound bacon
Flour for dredging scallops
1/2 cup real maple syrup
1/2 cup bread crumbs

Directions:
Fry bacon until crisp, drain on paper towels.
Reserve bacon grease in pan to cook scallops in. Crumble bacon.

Make pumpkin sauce.
Melt 2 tablespoons butter, add pumpkin and cream.
Bring to a boil.
Reduce to a simmer to keep warm while cooking scallops.

Heat bacon grease.
Dredge scallops in flour, then maple syrup, then bread crumbs.
Cook scallops 2 minutes per side in the bacon grease, over medium heat.
Spoon pumpkin sauce on a plate, add scallops, top with crumbled bacon.

Lasagna with Meat Sauce

Donna Doyen

My brother-in-law Mick absolutely loves this dish. I have been making this for him since his days in the Navy. He would always tease me that I should be a chef on a Navy ship.

Cook Time: 8 Hours
Yield: Large lasagna pan

Ingredients:

3 pounds lean hamburger

1 pound hot sausage meat

2 large yellow onions

10 cloves garlic pressed

2 quarts tomatoes

6-24 ounce cans Hunts herb and garlic sauce

2 tablespoons oregano

2 tablespoons basil

Mushrooms to taste, optional

Green pepper, chopped, optional

2 boxes lasagna noodles (not the no boil kind)

8 cups shredded Mozzarella cheese

1 pound Provolone cheese, each slice cut into 4 strips

5 ounces freshly grated Parmesan cheese

Loaf Italian or French bread depending on your preference

1/2 cup butter

2 garlic cloves, pressed

Directions:
Sauce: Can be made days ahead of time.
In large skillet heat 2 tablespoons olive oil, add chopped onion, green pepper, mushrooms, and half of the garlic. Cook until onions are translucent, then transfer to a large pot. In a skillet brown the meats, then add remainder of the pressed garlic cloves to the meat. Cook until no red remains. Drain off all the fat and discard. Add the meat into the large pot with the onions. Open the Hunts cans and add to the large pot. Add tomatoes and spices. Simmer all day or at least several hours.
When ready to assemble cook lasagna noodles, per directions and drain. In the lasagna pan layer sauce, noodles, sauce, Mozerella cheese, Provolone cheese, and about 2 tablespoons Parmesan cheese on top. Layer with noodles, sauce, and three cheeses, repeat until pan is full. Cover and bake foil covered at 350º, 45 minutes to 1 hour 15 minutes depending on the size of the pan. Let rest as you warm your bread for about 10 minutes.
Garlic bread: Mix garlic and butter. Cut the bread into slices, butter one side of each slice. Wrap in foil. Bake at 400º 10 minutes. Get the bread ready to go in the oven while the lasagna is cooking.

Notes: If making two pans freeze one before baking it with Saran Wrap on top then foil. Don't forget to take the Saran Wrap off before baking.

Baby Back Ribs

Donna Doyen

Cook Time: 275º 4 1/2 hours then grill
Yield: 3-4 racks of ribs

I would make these the day before going camping or boating and place them in Ziploc bags. We would bring them in a cooler with the BBQ sauce and just heat them up on the grill when we were ready for dinner. It makes for a quick easy dinner after setting up camp and gathering firewood. They will drive you crazy while they are cooking, they smell so good.

Ingredients:
Whole racks of baby back ribs
Salt
Pepper
Sweet Baby Ray's Barbecue Sauce or your favorite sauce.

Directions:
Peel the silver skin off the back of the ribs.
With a knife pull one edge up then grab it and pull it off the length of the rack of ribs and discard.
Season ribs with salt and pepper.
Place in a turkey roasting pan.
Cover tightly with heavy duty aluminum foil or lid.
Bake at 275º for 4 1/2 hours.
Either let cool, then place in Ziploc bags to heat up later or put BBQ sauce on them and return to the oven for 20 minutes or put them on the grill to sear.

Note:
If you are in a hurry, you can cook them in a pressure cooker. Cook at 10 pounds for 10 minutes.
Remove from the pressure cooker and season with BBQ sauce. Place in the oven at 350º 10-15 minutes or sear on a grill.

Beef Roast

We grew up eating meat and potatoes for dinner almost every night. My mother, Donilda (McKinney) Caron, loved to cook a roast in the oven along with some baked potatoes for an easy meal.

Cook Time: 475º for 15 minutes, reduce heat to 350º bake 15 minutes per pound.

Ingredients:
Top round sirloin roast
Olive oil
Pepper
Garlic powder
Onion powder
Basil

Directions:
Place roast on a rack in a foil lined pan.
Rub all sides with olive oil and spices.
Sear meat in a 475º oven for 15 minutes then turn down temperature to 350º, cook 15 minutes per pound.
For a medium-rare roast the internal temperature should be 130º.
Let rest, covered in foil 10-15 minutes.

Bone in Pork Roast

Donilda Caron

This recipe is a family favorite which my mother cooked once a week. She liked to cook roasts because they are delicious and easy. Pop it in the oven with some baked potatoes and you have dinner in a couple hours. Add a salad or a vegetable and you have a meal. Use the leftovers for a pork sandwich the next day. If you made gravy, the sandwich would be served hot; if not, it would be served cold with mustard.

Cook Time: 350º 1 1/2 - 2 1/2 hours depending on size
Yield: 6 Servings

Ingredients:
Pork roast-center cut
Garlic cloves, peeled
Lawry's seasoned salt

Directions:
Go to the butcher at the grocery store and request a "center cut pork roast." Figure out how many people you want to feed and add one rib. If feeding 6, ask for a seven rib, center cut pork roast. Ask them to cut the rib bone vertically between each rib (like a pork chop). This makes it easier to serve after it is cooked.
Preheat oven to 350º.
Cut slits in the fatty part of the meat and slide in the garlic cloves.
Sprinkle with Lawry's seasoned salt.
Insert a meat thermometer through the roast horizontally. Cook until the probe reaches 150º.
Remove from the oven, cover with foil and let rest for 10 to 15 minutes before carving.

Notes:
The most important part of this recipe is getting the roast at the supermarket. If you are in a rush, call ahead and ask for the meat department and it will be ready for you when you arrive. Bone-in meat will produce a more flavorful dish.

Chicken with Lemon and Rosemary
Megan McCollum

This is best cooked over a charcoal fire; however, I cook it in the oven during the winter.

Cook Time: Convection roast 325º 1 hour or bake 350º 1 hour to 1 hour 15 minutes. Marinate 1-2 days ahead. Two days is preferred.
Yield: Whole chicken

Ingredients:
Whole chicken, can cut in half or leave whole
3 lemons, zested and juiced, then put the used lemon halves in a Ziploc bag along with the zest and juice.
4-5 rosemary sprigs
Large bottle Ken's or Newman's Italian salad dressing
4 garlic cloves, cut in half
1 onion, cut up in chunks

Directions:
In a large freezer Ziploc bag, add all ingredients including the lemon after you squeeze out the juice.
Place bag in a bowl in case it leaks. Rotate it periodically.
Refrigerate at least 24 hours. It is better if you can marinate it two days!
Bake whole or cut in half and cook on a BBQ grill until internal temperature reaches 170º.

Notes:
Make two and freeze one.
This is very tasty and moist. If there are any leftovers, they make a great salad or sandwich. I usually do two whole chickens at a time.

Chicken with Sliced Almonds

Charlotte McCollum

This was a favorite of Uncle Jim, Charlotte's husband. When he had open heart surgery in the early 1980s, he completely changed his diet for the remainder of his life. Aunt Charlotte learned to cook chicken a hundred different ways. This recipe is one of her best chicken recipes.

Cook Time: 15 minutes stovetop
Yield: 4

Ingredients:
4 chicken breasts, pounded on the thick
    end to make it all the same thickness
1/4 cup butter
1 egg
1 teaspoon milk
1/2 cup flour
1 cup sliced almonds
Salt & pepper to taste

Directions:
Place flour, salt, and pepper in a shallow dish.
Place almonds on a plate.
Whisk egg and milk in a shallow dish.
Preheat butter in a skillet large enough to hold all the chicken breast.
Pound the thick part of the chicken breast until the entire breast is the same thickness.
Dredge chicken in the flour mixture, then egg mixture, then in the almonds. Sauté in the butter.
Cook 8 minutes per side on medium heat, until the chicken is cooked through.

Notes:
This is an elegant quick meal that has stood the test of time.

Chicken Orzo

Cook Time: 1 hour 10 minutes
Yield: 4

Ingredents:
Salt and pepper
2 -6 ounce chicken breasts
1 tablespoon olive oil
4 cups chicken broth
1 onion, minced
1 1/4 cups orzo
4 garlic cloves, minced
1/2 cup dry white wine
1 bunch asparagus, ends snipped
1/4 cup oil packed sundried tomatoes
1 cup grated Parmesan cheese
2 tablespoons fresh basil, chopped

Directions:
Pat chicken dry, season with salt and pepper.
Sear chicken in 2 teaspoons olive oil until golden brown.
Place chicken in pot with broth, simmer 18-25 minutes.
Shred or cut chicken into bite-size pieces.
Combine 1 teaspoon olive oil, onion, and 1/8 teaspoon salt in frying pan.
Cover and cook over medium- low heat until soft, 8-10 minutes.
Uncover, cook on medium-high heat until brown, 4-6 minutes.
Stir in orzo, cook over medium heat until lightly golden, 2-3 minutes.
Stir in garlic and wine, cook until evaporated.
Add broth and simmer until liquid is almost absorbed.
After 12-15 minutes, add asparagus, cook 10 minutes until tender crisp and orzo is creamy.
Remove from heat, add the chicken, sun-dried tomatoes, Parmesan cheese, and basil.

Chicken Piccata
Schari Roy

This recipe came about when Schari requested it for her birthday party. I found it easy and quick. It is great with baked stuffed potatoes or garlic potatoes. Yes, I love potatoes!

Cook Time: 200º 30 minutes
Yield: 4

Ingredients:
4 boneless skinless chicken breasts
Sea salt and ground pepper
Flour for dredging
6 tablespoons unsalted butter
5 tablespoons olive oil
1/3 cup fresh lemon juice
1/2 cup chicken broth
1/4 cup brined capers, rinsed
1/3 cup fresh parsley, chopped

Directions:
Preheat oven to 200º.
Slice chicken breasts in half horizontally.
Season chicken with salt and pepper, dredge in flour.
In a large skillet over medium high heat, melt 2 tablespoons butter and 3 tablespoons olive oil.
When it starts to sizzle, add 4 pieces of dredged chicken.
Cook 3 minutes, flip chicken over, cook 3 more minutes.
When browned, remove to an oven safe plate, keep warm in a 200º degree oven.
Melt 2 tablespoons butter and 2 tablespoons olive oil, repeat with remainder of chicken.
When all the chicken is cooked, add lemon juice, chicken broth, and capers to the pan.
Bring to a boil, add the chicken to the pan to coat both sides.
Remove to a serving platter.
Add 2 tablespoons butter to the sauce, whisk vigorously.
Pour over the chicken and serve topped with parsley.

Crab potatoes, "Crab Unique"
Lisa Mitchell

Lisa is my best friend from high school days. We worked together and went to college together as well. She made this for us while visiting from Massachusetts. She served this with ribeye steak. I immediately wrote this recipe in my journal as I knew it was a "keeper!"

Cook Time: 375º 1 hour 15 minutes
Yield: 6

Ingredients:
1 pound crab meat
1 tablespoon grated onion
2 tablespoons butter
4 tablespoons milk
1/4 teaspoon red cayenne pepper
6 medium potatoes
1/2 teaspoon salt
1/2 cup cheddar cheese, grated

Directions:
Preheat oven to 375º.
Bake potatoes 1 hour.
Scrape out potato and place in bowl with all ingredients except cheese. Mix.
Re-stuff potatoes, top with cheese.
Bake until warm and cheese melts, 10-15 minutes.

Lobster Potato Salad

Donna Doyen

There is never a shortage of ways to use up leftover lobster meat. Just a little mayonnaise and a drizzle of melted butter on a good roll or just dipped in cocktail sauce for an appetizer. However this recipe can stretch two cups of lobster to feed six and no one will feel deprived! Cook a "red snapper," (Maine hot dog), on the grill and you have yourself a meal.

Cook Time: 30 minutes, total cooking time, chill at least 1 hour
Yield: serves 6

Ingredients:

2 cups lobster, cooked, cleaned and chilled
5 cups potatoes, cooked, diced and chilled
1/3 cup green onion, thinly sliced
1 teaspoon salt
1/2 teaspoon pepper
1/3 cup celery, chopped
2/3 cup Hellmann's Mayonnaise
2 teaspoons lemon juice, freshly squeezed
2 teaspoons prepared horseradish
1 teaspoon dry mustard
1/4 to 1/2 teaspoon cayenne pepper, to taste
4 Hard-boiled eggs, cut into wedges to garnish the top
Romaine lettuce leaves washed and chilled, to place under the potato salad for presentation, optional

Directions:
Place chopped lobster in a bowl, reserving claws for a garnish.
Add potatoes, onion, celery, salt, pepper and toss lightly.
In a small bowl mix mayonnaise, lemon juice, horseradish, mustard and cayenne. Pour over lobster potato mixture. Toss lightly.
Refrigerate at least one hour.
To serve, fan out romaine leaves on a platter or large salad bowl.
Spoon salad on top, garnish with claws and egg wedges.

Roasted Cauliflower
Sherry Fletcher

Cook Time: 450º 30 min

Ingredients:
3 tablespoons olive oil
1 1/2 teaspoons cumin
1 1/2 teaspoons coriander
1/4 teaspoon kosher salt
1/4 teaspoon pepper
1 cauliflower, cut in 2 inch florets
Lemon wedges

Directions:
Preheat oven to 450º.
Whisk oil and seasoning in a large bowl.
Toss in cauliflower.
Place on a large baking pan.
Roast at 450º for 30 minutes, turn over half way through.
Season with lemon.

Baked Stuffed Loaded Potatoes
Megan McCollum

In the summer we often eat dinner with our cousins Bruce and Megan. Several times a summer Megan will make these potatoes and they are always a huge hit. Half a potato per person is usually enough, but make extra as they are almost as good the next day! These go great with a thick steak cooked on the grill and a salad. (And rum cake for dessert).

Cook Time: 400º 45 to 60 minutes plus 30 minutes after stuffing
Yield: serves 8

Ingredients:
4 large russet potatoes, washed and poked with a fork
2 cups freshly grated cheddar cheese (I use my food processor)
3 tablespoons butter, melted
1/2 to 3/4 cup sour cream or plain yogurt
3-4 scallions cut up including the greens
4 pieces thick cut bacon fried crispy, then crumbled
Salt & pepper to taste

Directions:
Bake the potatoes in a 400º oven until the skin is crispy but the potato is still a bit firm, about 45-60 minutes.
Using an oven mitt, cut the potatoes in half lengthwise. Scoop the flesh into a large bowl, leaving it chunky. To the potato flesh add a cup of shredded cheddar cheese, most of the scallions, reserving some greens for the top, and the sour cream or plain yogurt. Gently stir.
Meanwhile line a cookie sheet with foil. Place the potato skins on the cookie sheet and brush them with about a teaspoon of melted butter on each half. Sprinkle with salt and pepper return to the oven for 5-10 minutes until they crisp up.
Restuff the shells, topping with bacon bits, more cheddar cheese, and the scallion greens. Set aside.
30 minutes before dinner is ready, return stuffed potatoes to preheated oven.
Bake at 350º for 30 minutes until heated through and cheese is melted.

 96

Desserts

Grandma's McKinney's Pie Crust
Irene McKinney

I grew up standing on a chair in my grandmother's kitchen "helping" her make pies. I would grab a piece of dough and eat it raw. She would sigh and say, "Oh; stop that, you are going to get worms eating raw dough!" It didn't stop me. She would let me have the scraps to make a mini pie for myself or a "pig's ear," which was dough rolled out spread with butter, sugar, and cinnamon rolled into a log and baked. I have fond memories of her every time I bake a pie. Pie crust need not be intimidating. It may take a few tries to get it right but keep trying. The key to a flaky crust is not to overwork the dough and add ice water a little at a time to achieve the right consistency.

Cook Time: 400º 20 minutes when a recipe calls for a prebaked shell.
Yield: 2 crusts for one large deep dish pie or two pie shells

Ingredients:
3 cups four
1 cup Crisco
1 teaspoon salt
1 teaspoon sugar
Ice water

Directions:
Mix flour, salt, and sugar with fingers, add Crisco, mix with hands until the Crisco has broken down to the size of peas.
Add ice water just until the dough holds together while stirring with fingers.
Divide dough in half.
Roll out on floured piece of wax paper with a floured rolling pin.
Lift wax paper and dough and flip over on to the pie plate.
Remove wax paper.
Crimp edges.

Notes:
If prebaking a pie shell, place holes in the dough with a fork. Bake at 400º for 15 to 20 minutes until light brown.

Old Fashioned Rhubarb Pie
Avis Black

This is an old Maine recipe from my husband's cousin, Avis Harkness Black of Veazie, Maine. Avis loved rhubarb and would grow it beside her garage. When I first made this pie, I fell in love with it. It is tart and has a custard-like center. You will not miss the strawberries!

Cook Time: 1 hour: 450° 15 minutes, reduce heat to 350°, cook 45 minutes
Yield: 8 slices

Ingredients:
Grandma's Pie Crust recipe, page 98
6 cups rhubarb
1 1/2 cups sugar
4 1/2 tablespoons flour
2 beaten eggs
1 1/2 tablespoons butter softened

Directions:
Preheat oven to 450°.
In a large bowl mix rhubarb, sugar, eggs, flour, and butter.
Roll out crust and place into a deep dish 9 inch pie plate, pour in the rhubarb mixture.
Roll out second crust.
Cut crust into 1 inch wide strips.
Weave a lattice pattern on top of the rhubarb.
Bake at 450° 15 minutes, reduce heat to 350° bake for 45 minutes.

No Bake Blueberry Pie
Robin Ouellette

My girls like this hot, but it is supposed to be served chilled. Sometimes you just can't wait for a good thing!

Cook Time: 30 minutes
Yield: 8 slices

Ingredients:
1 precooked pie crust 9 inch deep dish see recipe, page 98
5 cups blueberries
3/4 cup sugar
2 tablespoons cornstarch
Whip cream or Cool Whip

Directions:
In a heavy saucepan put 2 1/2 cups blueberries, sugar, and cornstarch.
Heat over med-low heat until it boils stirring constantly.
Put remainder of blueberries in a precooked pie shell.
When berries and sugar come to a boil, pour over raw berries in the shell.
Place Saran Wrap on top of the pie and refrigerate.
Serve chilled with whipped cream or Cool Whip.

Strawberry Rhubarb Pie

Donna Doyen

I grew up eating rhubarb from a neighbor's garden as I walked home from school in Vermont. I can't wait to see the first curls of rhubarb breaking the surface in spring. I made a border of rhubarb around my garden because I heard it kept animals out (an old wives tail that doesn't work). However it gives me plenty of rhubarb to use all summer. When I see about two inches of stalk, I start harvesting; patience is not one of my strong suits.

Cook Time: 400º 15 minutes reduce to 350º 45 minutes
Yield: 8 slices

Ingredients:
Grandma's pie crust recipe, page 98
5 cups strawberries hulled, big ones cut in half
3 cups rhubarb, cut in 1 inch pieces
1 cup sugar
3 tablespoons flour
1 teaspoon cinnamon
1/4 teaspoon nutmeg, optional
1 tablespoon butter
Vanilla ice cream

Directions:
In a large bowl mix strawberries and rhubarb.
In a separate bowl mix sugar, flour, and spices, mix and pour over berries, stir.
Line a 9 inch deep dish pie plate with a crust, add berry mixture, dot with butter, add top crust, and crimp edges.
Decorate top crust with steam holes.
Bake at 400º for 15 minutes, reduce heat to 350º bake 45 minutes.
Serve with vanilla ice cream.

Pumpkin Pie
Irene McKinney

This is my grandmother's recipe. I won first place at the Blue Hill Peninsula Food and Wine Festival in 2013 with this recipe. We always had this pie at family holiday parties, along with apple, berry and whatever grandma decided to make. We could never have too much pie, as she would feed it to anyone who stopped in, along with a cup of coffee that was always percolating on her wood stove.

Cook Time: 425º 15 minutes reduce to 350º 45 minutes
Yield: 8

Ingredients:
Grandma's pie crust recipe, page 98
2 eggs
1 can or 2 cups cooked sugar pumpkin
3/4 cup sugar
1/2 teaspoon salt
1 teaspoon cinnamon
1/2 teaspoon ginger
1/2 teaspoon nutmeg
1/4 teaspoon ground cloves
1 2/3 cups evaporated milk,
        I add regular milk to top off one can
1/8 cup molasses, (2 tablespoons)
1-9 inch pie shell, not baked

Directions:
Preheat oven to 425º.
Beat eggs, add rest of ingredients, whisk, and pour into unbaked pie shell.
Sprinkle with nutmeg.
Bake 15 minutes at 425º then reduce heat to 350º, bake 45 minutes longer until knife inserted in the middle comes out clean.
Serve with whipped cream.

Peanut Butter Pie

Donna Doyen

Smooth and creamy.
This is one of my husband's favorites. It is good any time of year and so easy to make but not easy to keep, as it has a way of disappearing once it is discovered. This recipe is especially tasty on a hot summer evening.

Cook Time: none
Yield: 8 slices

Ingredients:
4 ounces cream cheese, softened
1/2 cup smooth peanut butter
1 cup confectioners sugar
8 ounces Cool Whip, thawed
1/2 cup milk
Oreo crust, I usually use a store bought one with a lid
Fudge sauce to decorate plate, optional
Chocolate curls, optional

Directions:
Beat cream cheese, peanut butter, confectioners sugar and milk until smooth.
Fold in Cool Whip.
Pour into Oreo crust.
Cover with plastic lid from store bought crust.
Freeze.

Blueberry Pie
Donna Doyen

This recipe won first place in the Blue Hill Fair in 2013.
When I was dating my husband, he said he would bring me some winnowed blueberries. He asked me if I knew what raked and winnowed blueberries were. I didn't want to appear ignorant so, I replied "yes." I went on to tell my coworkers that I would make a blueberry pie for work the next day. Well, being the procrastinator that I am, I did not clean the blueberries until the next morning before work. I started picking the blueberries over one at a time and it took forever. The hour that I planned on baking the pie was spent cleaning leaves, green berries, and stems out of the blueberries! I knew I had to bring in a pie to work, so I made it, and brought it in raw. I cooked it at work and it was devoured within minutes.

Cook Time: Convection bake 375º 45 minutes or bake 400º 15 minutes
reduce heat to 350º 45 minutes
Yield: 8 pieces

Ingredients:
Grandma's Pie Crust recipe, page 98
6 cups blueberries fresh or frozen
      (if using frozen berries do not thaw)
3 tablespoons flour
1 tablespoon cornstarch
1 scant cup sugar
2 teaspoons cinnamon
Zest of 1 lemon
1 tablespoon lemon juice
Rhubarb*, see note

Directions:
Preheat oven to convection bake 375º
Add lemon juice and zest to the blueberries.
In a large bowl mix flour, sugar, cornstarch, and cinnamon.
Add to the blueberries, stir, let sit 15 minutes, while you make the pie crust for a two-crust pie.
Stir the berries and sugar, pour into the pie shell.
Roll out another crust and place it on top of the berries.
Crimp the edges and cut decorative steam holes in the top crust.
Bake as directed.

Notes:

Winnowed blueberries are berries that have been raked, usually by hand then put through a winnowing machine to blow out most leaves and grass but still need to be handpicked over, which can be time consuming.

Personally, I don't care for plain blueberry pie. I like mine tart and like to make my filling with 3 cups blueberries and 3 cups rhubarb! (No need for the lemon).

Apple Cranberry Pie
Donna Doyen

I also won first place at the Blue Hill Peninsula Food and Wine Festival with this pie in 2013. When I see local farmers and fishermen on the side of the road selling their seafood and produce, I can't resist the urge to purchase some of their harvest. In the fall they sell fresh cranberries, all clean in Ziploc bags. I can't wait to add them in my favorite recipes to give them a new twist with some zing.

Cook Time: Convection bake 375º 45 minutes or regular bake 400º 15 minutes, reduce heat to 350º 35-45 minutes more.
Yield: 8 slices

Ingredients:
Grandma's pie crust or your favorite pie crust recipe, page 98
6 cups apples, 2 each Granny Smith, Cortland, and Macintosh
2 cups fresh or frozen cranberries
2 teaspoons cinnamon
1/2 teaspoon nutmeg
3/4 cup sugar
2 tablespoons flour
1 tablespoon butter

Directions:
Peel and core, apples, cut each quarter into thirds.
Place in a large bowl. In a separate bowl mix sugar, spices, and flour.
Pour over apples, add cranberries, and stir.
Preheat oven.
Make grandma's pie crust.
In a 9 inch deep dish pie plate put one crust in the bottom, add apple mixture, dot with butter, place top crust on, crimp the edges and make decorative steam holes in the top crust.
Bake.

Slush Cake

Valerie Legare

My Aunt Valerie would always visit with stuffed cabbage rolls and slush cake. As a child I would only eat the slush cake. When I was 18, I visited her in Washington State and learned how to make the stuffed cabbage rolls and discovered I loved them as much as my mother did. I have been making them for my mother ever since. My husband, Phil and our daughter, Katherine like the Slush Cake as their birthday cake!

Cook Time: 350° 30 minutes, refrigerate 6 hours.
Yield: 9X13 pan

Ingredients:

Crust:
1 cup flour
1/2 cup butter, melted
1/2 cup chopped walnuts

Cream cheese layer:
1 pound cream cheese, softened
1 cup confectioners sugar
1 1/2 cups Cool Whip

Chocolate layer:
3-1.3 ounce packages Jell-O Cook and Serve
    chocolate pudding
5 cups milk

Topping:
8 ounce container Cool Whip,
Walnuts, chopped

Directions:
Place the milk in a large saucepan and whisk in the pudding packets. Stir constantly until it comes to a boil. Place a sheet of plastic wrap right on the pudding to prevent a skin from forming. Cool.
Preheat oven to 350°.
Prepare crust in a 9X13 pan. Mix flour, butter, and nuts together with your hands and press to the edges of the pan. It will be a thin crust. Bake at 350° for 15 minutes. Cool.
In a bowl, beat the cream cheese with 1 cup of confectioners sugar, and 1 1/2 cups of Cool Whip with a hand mixer. Pour over the cooled crust.
When the pudding has cooled, pour over the cream cheese layer.
Top with Cool Whip, and nuts.
Cover with plastic wrap. Refrigerate at least 6 hours.

Blueberry Cake with Lemon Sauce
Elizabeth Doyen (Phil's mom)

My mother-in-law made this the first time I met her and it has been one of my favorites ever since. Our daughter Karen always had this as her birthday cake. I would have to make a chocolate cake as well, because most of the other kids would look at this in puzzlement, wondering where the frosting was.

Cook Time: 350º 50-60 minutes
Yield: 8X8 pan.

Ingredients:
1 1/2 cups flour, save out 1 teaspoon for
    dusting blueberries
2 eggs, separated
1/2 cup Crisco
1 cup sugar
1/4 teaspoon salt
1 teaspoon vanilla
1/3 cup milk
1 teaspoon baking powder
1 1/2 cups blueberries, fresh or frozen

Lemon sauce:
1/2 cup butter, melted
1 cup sugar
1/4 cup water
1 egg, beaten well
Juice of 1 lemon (3 tablespoons), zest of a lemon

Directions:
Preheat oven to 350º.
Beat egg whites until stiff, gradually add 1/4 cup sugar, set aside.
Cream Crisco with salt and vanilla, gradually add remainder 3/4 cup sugar.
Sift dry ingredients, set aside 1 teaspoon of flour.
Add sifted dry ingredients to the Crisco mixture alternating with milk.
Dust the berries with 1 teaspoon of flour.
Fold egg whites into batter, fold in blueberries.
Grease and flour pan, add batter, bake at 350º for 50-60 minutes until toothpick comes out clean.

Lemon sauce:
In a heavy saucepan add melted butter, sugar, water, egg, and lemon juice. Whisk well. Turn heat on to medium-high and bring to a boil. Remove from heat and strain. Add lemon zest, stir. Serve over warm cake.
Double the recipe for a 9X13 pan.

Rum Cake

Charlotte McCollum

This is a family favorite! It is so easy to make and is always a hit when we take it to a gathering. Uncle Jim, Charlotte's husband, would pour a shot rum on top of his cake when he ate it! The rest of us are perfectly happy with the rum glaze.

Cook Time: 350º 50-60 minutes
Yield: 1 bundt cake

Cake ingredients:
1 cup chopped walnuts or pecans. I use pecans; my daughter Beth only uses walnuts.
1- 18 ounce box yellow cake mix
1-1 ounce box vanilla instant pudding mix
4 eggs or egg beaters
1/2 cup cold water
1/2 cup oil
1/2 cup dark rum

Glaze ingredients:
1/2 cup butter
1/4 cup water
1 cup sugar
1/2 cup dark rum

Directions:
Grease and flour a tube pan. Sprinkle nuts on the bottom.
Mix all other cake ingredients together in a bowl. Pour on top of nuts in tube pan.
Bake at 350º 50-60 minutes.
Cool 10 minutes in the pan, invert on a cooling rack. Cool completely.

Glaze:
Do not make ahead of time.
Melt butter, stir in water and sugar. Bring to a rolling boil. Boil 5 minutes stirring constantly. Remove from heat, add rum.
Put cake nut side down on a platter. Poke holes in the cake with a fork or meat thermometer. Drizzle glaze on cake unitl it is all absorbed.

Blueberry Buckle
Ann Shafer

This recipe, loaded with blueberries, came from my husband's mother, Elizabeth; however, she was not known for making it often. Mrs. Shafer would make it for breakfast and dessert. When we were camping with our small children before building our house, Ann and Bill Shafer would invite us for dinner. They would serve this for dessert and send us home with the rest of the buckle for our breakfast. It tasted delicious in the morning with a hot tea!

Cook Time: 350º 50-60 minutes
Yeild: 8X8 pan. Double recipe for 9X13 pan.

Ingredients:
1/4 cup butter, softened
3/4 cup sugar
1 egg
2 cups flour (save out 1 teaspoon flour to toss with blueberries)
2 teaspoons baking powder
1/2 teaspoon salt
1/2 cup milk
2 cups blueberries

Topping:
1/4 cup cold butter
1/2 rounded cup sugar
1/3 rounded cup flour
1 teaspoon cinnamon

Directions:
Preheat oven to 350º. Grease and flour 8X8 baking pan.
Cream butter and sugar until light and fluffy.
Add egg, beat well, add dry ingredients and milk. Beat until incorporated.
Toss 1 teaspoon flour with blueberries. Fold in berries. Batter will be stiff.
Put in pan.

Make topping:
Mix dry ingredients, cut in butter.
Spread on top of cake.
Bake at 350º 45-50 minutes until toothpick comes out clean.

Lemon Pudding Cakes

Cook Time: 350º 20-25 minutes
Yield: 8 servings

Ingredients:
1 cup sugar, divided
1/3 cup flour
3 eggs, room temperature
1 cup skim milk
2 teaspoons grated lemon zest
1/2 cup fresh lemon juice
2 tablespoons butter, melted, plus extra for the custard cups

Directions:
Preheat oven to 350º.
Boil a kettle of water.
Butter 8 custard cups or ramekins, 1/2-3/4 cup size.
Place ramekins in a deep baking dish that can accommodate water half way up the ramekins.
Separate egg yolks from whites. In a medium bowl whisk 3/4 cup sugar and flour.
Whisk in egg yolks, milk, butter, lemon zest, and lemon juice.
In a separate bowl with a hand mixer beat egg whites until they form soft peaks.
Beat in 1/4 cup sugar until they become thick and glossy. Fold the egg whites into the lemon batter. Divide the batter among the 8 ramekins.
Add boiling water to the pan until it comes halfway up the sides of the ramekins.
Bake until the cakes become golden brown and start to pull away from the sides, about 20-25 minutes. Remove from oven, cool on a rack, serve warm or room temperature.

Note:
The Lemon Pudding Cakes taste great plain or with Blueberry Compote on top. See page 123

 111

Carrot Cake

Karen Caron

This cake has been a family favorite for years. However my children do not like nuts in their cake so I would make sure half of the cake had nuts and half without nuts. I had to be careful to line them up when I frosted it.

Cook Time: 350º 45 minutes. Make a day ahead.
Yield: 2 layer cake

Ingredients:
2 cups flour
2 cups sugar
2 teaspoons baking soda
2 teaspoons cinnamon
1 teaspoon vanilla
1 cup oil
4 eggs
3 cups carrots, shredded
1/2 cup walnuts, chopped

Frosting:
1/2 cup butter, softened
8 ounces cream cheese, softened
1 teaspoon vanilla
1 pound box 10X confectioners sugar

Directions:
Preheat oven to 350º.
Grease and flour 2, 9 inch pans.
In a large bowl, sift flour, sugar, baking soda, and cinnamon.
Add eggs, carrots, and vanilla.
Fold in walnuts. Pour into 2 pans.
Bake at 350º, 45 minutes.

Frosting:
Combine all ingredients.
Mix on high until smooth.
Frost cake, store overnight in refrigerator for best flavor.

Notes:
Tip: To get both cakes the same size, weigh the batter in the baking pans on a kitchen scale and adjust as necessary.

Blueberry Slump

Maria Messier

Living in Maine we can buy blueberries in 30 pound boxes from the blueberry processor. When making this recipe, you will be glad you didn't have to pick 10 cups by hand!

Cook Time: 400º 25 minutes
Yield: 9X13 pan

Ingredients:
10 cups blueberries
1 1/2 cups sugar, divided
1/2 cup water, use 1/4 cup if berries are frozen
3 tablespoons cornstarch, dissolved in 3 tablespoons water
2-8 ounce packages cream cheese, softened
1/2 teaspoon vanilla
1 1/2 tablespoons lemon juice

Biscuit:
1 1/2 cups flour
1/3 cup brown sugar
1 tablespoon baking powder
1/4 teaspoon salt
3/4 cup milk
3 tablespoons butter, melted
Vanilla ice cream

Directions:
Preheat oven to 400º.
In a large saucepan, bring berries, 1 cup plus 2 tablespoons sugar and either 1/4 or 1/2 cup water depending if your berries are frozen or not, to a boil, stirring frequently.
Add cornstarch mixture, stir until thickened.
Pour into a 9X13 baking pan, cool to room temperature, or it will curdle.
With a hand mixer beat cream cheese, 6 tablespoons sugar, lemon juice, and vanilla until smooth.
Drop by the spoonful over cooled berries, spacing evenly. Do not spread.

Biscuit:
Mix together dry ingredients, stir in milk and butter.
Drop by the spoonful over cream cheese layer, do not spread.
Bake until filling bubbles and biscuit browns. Approximately 25 minutes.
Cool slightly.
Great with ice cream or Cool Whip.

Chocolate Fudgy Truffle Cheesecake
Donna Doyen

Phil cannot leave this cheesecake alone. He used to say, "I don't like cheesecake." I think he has changed his mind now. This cheesecake is very impressive and feeds a crowd. It is well worth the investment of a 12 inch spring form pan.

Cook Time: 350º 1hour 10 minutes.
　　　　　Bake a day ahead.
Yield: 12 inch spring form pan

Ingredients:
Crust:
1-9 ounce package of Nabisco
"Famous Chocolate Wafers" or Oreo cookies
6 tablespoons butter, melted

Filling:
6-8 ounce packages cream cheese, softened
2 cups sugar
1 1/2 teaspoon vanilla
6 eggs
3 cups semi-sweet chocolate chips, melted

Topping:
1/2 cup semi-sweet chocolate chips, melted
1/3 cup evaporated milk
1 pint fresh raspberries
3 tablespoons powdered sugar, optional

Directions:

Preheat oven to 350º.

In a food processor with a metal blade, crush wafers, add melted butter, process until smooth. Press crust to the bottom of a spring form pan or for individual servings in a paper-lined muffin tin. Bake 10 minutes.

In a large bowl, beat cream cheese and sugar until smooth, add eggs one at a time beating until incorporated. Blend in melted chocolate and vanilla. Then stir a few times with a rubber spatula to blend the chocolate evenly. Pour into prepared crust. Boil a teapot of water and pour into a separate baking pan. Place baking pan with water on oven shelf under the cheesecake.

Bake at 350º 1 hour 10 minutes until just set. It should jiggle slightly in the middle when gently shaken.

If making individual cheesecakes in a muffin tin, bake at 375º 15-20 minutes.

Topping:

When the cheesecake has cooled, melt 1/2 cup chocolate chips, add evaporated milk and stir until smooth.

Remove outside ring from pan and drizzle topping all over top and sides of cheesecake. Serve topped with fresh raspberries.

Notes:

Half the recipe for a 9 inch spring form pan. Put a pan of boiling water on the shelf, under the cheesecake during cooking for a smooth top.

Bake at 300º for 55-60 minutes.

Rhubarb Cheesecake

Maria Messier

While in college our daughter Elizabeth would make bets using this cheesecake as her wager. If she lost, she got to eat cheesecake with her friends. Win, win!

Cook Time: 350º 30 minutes, chill 2 hours
Yield: 8 slices

Ingredients:
1 1/4 cups graham cracker crumbs
1/4 cup butter, melted
1 1/4 cups sugar, divided
3 tablespoons cornstarch
4 cups rhubarb, cut in 1 inch pieces
8 ounces cream cheese, softened
2 eggs
1/2 teaspoon vanilla
1 cup sour cream

Directions:
In a food processor with chopping blade, add graham crackers pulse, add 1 tablespoon sugar and melted butter, pulse, until chopped fine.
Press in springform pan (9 or 10 inch).
Bake at 300º for 10 minutes or use a premade crust transferred to a spring form pan.
In a saucepan mix 3/4 cup sugar, cornstarch, rhubarb and 1 tablespoon water. Stir often over medium heat until mixture comes to a boil.
Pour into crust.
With a mixer blend cream cheese and 6 tablespoons of sugar until smooth, add eggs and vanilla, mix just until combined.
Pour over rhubarb.
Bake at 350º for 20 minutes.
Mix sour cream with 1 tablespoon sugar, spread over the hot filling, bake five additional minutes.
Cool.
Refrigerate at least 2 hours.

Strawberry Rhubarb Crisp
Donna Doyen

Our kids don't like nuts in desserts so I usually put topping on half, then add the nuts and sprinkle on the other half. More nuts for those who like them.

Cook Time: 375º 35-45 minutes
Yield: Lasagna pan full

Ingredients:
11 cups rhubarb, cut in 1 inch pieces
1 1/2 quarts strawberries
1 cup plus 1/3 cup flour
1 1/2 teaspoons cinnamon
1/2 cup butter, cold, cut up
1 cup light brown sugar, packed
1 cup old fashioned oats
3/4 cup pecans, coarsely chopped

Directions:
Butter a large baking dish or lasagna pan.
Combine rhubarb, strawberries, sugar, 1/3 cup flour, and cinnamon.
Mix well and pour into baking dish.

Topping:
Combine 1 cup flour, 1 cup brown sugar, oats, and cut up butter.
Add pecans.
Sprinkle on top.
Bake at 375º 35-45 minutes.

Oatmeal Cookies

This recipe was in the Ellsworth American, a local newspaper. I made it, loved it, and then lost it. I drove to the newspaper office and asked for help some six months later. A young lady found it for me again and the next time I went to town I delivered her a batch of these delicious cookies. She commented, "This is the first time anyone has ever done this!"

Cook Time: 350° 9-12 minutes until lightly brown

Ingredients:
1 cup raisins soaked in boiling water, removed from the heat. Drain when soft.
3 eggs well beaten
1 teaspoon vanilla
1 cup butter, softened
1 cup brown sugar, packed
1 cup sugar
2 1/2 cups flour
1 teaspoon salt
1 teaspoon cinnamon
2 teaspoons baking soda
2 cups oatmeal, old fashioned
3/4 cup pecans, chopped

Directions:
In a large bowl combine drained raisins, eggs and vanilla, cover with plastic wrap, let stand 1 HOUR!
In another bowl, cream the butter and sugars.
Add flour, salt, cinnamon and baking soda.
Mix well, blend in egg and raisin mixture, oatmeal and nuts. Dough will be stiff.
Drop by heaping teaspoons onto ungreased cookie sheets.
Bake at 350° 9-12 minutes until edges are lightly browned.

Chocolate Cake
Priscilla York

This cake is so moist and delicious. Priscilla would make me this cake whenever I asked her to. She refused to give out the recipe because the recipients of it didn't follow the directions and would use other cocoa or oil than specified. Once our first daughter Karen was turning one, I pleaded with Priscilla to get her recipe. I agreed to make it as is, and it quickly became a family favorite. It actually gets better with age! If you can keep it a day!

Cook Time: 350° 20-25 minutes
Yield: 2 layer cake 9 inch

Ingredients:
Cake:
3 cups flour
1/2 cup Hershey's cocoa powder
2 cups sugar
2 teaspoons baking soda
2 cups tap water
2/3 cup Wesson oil
2 teaspoons vanilla
2 teaspoons white vinegar

Frosting:
7 rounded tablespoons Hershey's cocoa powder
2 pounds confectioners sugar, sifted
1/2 cup butter, softened
1 teaspoon vanilla
2 tablespoons ++ water

Directions:
Preheat oven to 350°.
In a large bowl sift dry ingredients. Add remainder of cake ingredients and beat until smooth.
Grease and flour two round tins, line the bottom with parchment paper. Pour the batter into the tins; you can weigh them to get them even, or just eyeball it.
Tap the tins to get the air out and spread batter to the edges.
Bake until the cake starts to pull away from the pan and toothpick comes out clean, 20-25 minutes.
Invert on a cooling rack, pull off the parchment paper and discard.

Make frosting:
Sift sugar and cocoa in a large bowl. Add butter and vanilla.
Add 2 tablespoons of water and beat. Slowly add more water by the teaspoon, until the frosting is spreadable.

Donna's Pantry
Sauces, Jams, and Candy

Blueberry Sauce
Elizabeth Doyen (Phil's mother)

This has so many uses-over pancakes or waffles, over ice cream or egg crêpes. On top of blueberry blintzes. You get the idea. We love our blueberries!

Cook Time: 5 min
Yield: 3 cups

Blueberry sauce ingredients:
3 cups blueberries
6 tablespoons sugar
2 1/2 teaspoons cornstarch
2 tablespoons water
1 tablespoon lemon juice
Zest of 1 lemon

Directions:
Dissolve the cornstarch in the water.
Put all ingredients in a heavy saucepan, bring to a boil, stirring constantly until thickened.

Lemon Curd
Terence Janericco

Ingredients:
4 egg yolks
3/4 cup sugar

3 ounces lemon juice
4 tablespoons butter, melted
Pinch of salt
2 teaspoons lemon zest

Directions:
In sauce pan, beat yolks and sugar with whisk until well blended.
Stir in lemon juice, butter and salt.
Cook over medium-low heat until it coats the back of a metal spoon. Stirring constantly.
Strain, then add lemon zest.

Blueberry Compote

Ingredients:
1 tablespoon butter
2 cups blueberries
2 tablespoons sugar
Pinch salt
1/2 teaspoon lemon juice

Directions:
Melt butter in sauce pan.
Add berries, sugar, and salt.
Bring to a boil.
Reduce heat to simmer for 8-10 minutes.
Remove pan from heat.
Add lemon juice.

Caramel Sauce

Cook Time: 10 minutes

Ingredients:
1 cup brown sugar
1/2 cup half and half
4 tablespoons butter
Pinch salt
1 tablespoon vanilla

Directions:
Mix sugar, half and half, butter, and salt in a heavy saucepan.
Whisk 5 to 7 minutes over medium heat.
Add vanilla, cook 1 additional minute.
Cool, store in refrigerator.

Charlotte's Hot Fudge Sauce
Charlotte McCollum

Uncle Jim, Charlotte's husband, liked rum on everything-even his ice cream.

Ingredients:
4 ounces unsweetened Baker's chocolate or 1 cup cocoa powder plus 4 tablespoons oil
3 tablespoons butter
2/3 cup boiling water
1 2/3 cups sugar
6 tablespoons corn syrup (a scant 1/2 cup)
1 tablespoon dark rum

Directions:
Melt chocolate and butter slowly. Heat water to boiling and add to chocolate, mix well. Add sugar and corn syrup, mix until smooth, bring to a boil stirring constantly. Reduce heat to very low and bring to a rolling boil for 9 minutes without stirring. Remove from heat. Let cool 15 minutes then add 1 tablespoon of dark rum.

....

Helen's Hot Fudge Sauce
Helen Martin Orth

Helen served this fudge on top of coffee ice cream.
She liked to scoop coffee ice cream into a muffin tin, top with toasted crushed pecans, and put in the freezer.
Take out and top with the hot fudge sauce.

Ingredients:
1 can sweetened condensed milk
3 ounces unsweetened baker's chocolate
1 teaspoon vanilla

Directions:
Melt chocolate, add milk and vanilla.
Enjoy.

Rhubarb Sauce

This sauce is so tangy and good. I put it on top of waffles, pancakes, crêpes, cheesecake, and ice cream. Some of our southern guests have never had rhubarb.

Ingredients:
2 tablespoons butter
4 cups rhubarb
1/2 cup sugar
Sometimes I add some strawberries

Directions:
In a heavy saucepan bring all ingredients to a boil over medium-high heat, stirring constantly 5-10 minutes, until rhubarb is soft.

Raspberry Sauce

Ingredients:
3 cups raspberries fresh or frozen
1 teaspoon fresh lemon juice
2 tablespoons confectioners sugar

Directions:
Place all ingredients in a high-speed blender or Vitamix and process until smooth.
Strain through a fine mesh strainer.
Refrigerate.

Hollandaise Sauce

Yield: 1 1/2 cups

Ingredients:
4 large egg yolks
2 tablespoons fresh lemon juice
Salt and pepper to taste
1 cup unsalted butter, melted

Directions:
In a blender, combine egg yolks, lemon juice, salt, and pepper.
In a small saucepan melt the butter. With the blender running, slowly add the warm butter through the vent in the lid.
Blend until thick and smooth. Serve immediately.

Note: If too thick the sauce can be thinned with a little water.

Strawberry Rhubarb Jam
Donna Doyen

Growing up, I loved making jam. My grandmother would have hot biscuits and with the extra jam that didn't fit in the jar, we would spoon it on the biscuits and eat it right away. Making jam was the one thing my grandfather would take charge of in the kitchen. He loved jam on his saltine crackers.

Ingredients:
2 cups strawberries, hulled and mashed
2 cups rhubarb, cut up
5 1/2 cups sugar
1 box sure jell
1/2 teaspoon butter

Directions:
Run jars through the dishwasher.
Bring your canner or large pot of water to a boil.
Heat 1 cup water to boiling, place flat lids in water, remove from heat.
Put fruit in a large heavy pot.
Measure sugar and set aside.
Add 1 box sure jell and 1/2 teaspoon butter to the fruit.
Turn heat to high and bring to a full rolling boil stirring constantly.
Add sugar, return to a full rolling boil. Boil exactly 1 minute.
Remove from heat, skim off any foam.
Working quickly fill all the jars.
Wipe the rims of the jars. Put the lids on finger tight.
Lower jars into canner of boiling water. Make sure water covers the lids by 1-2 inches.
Bring to a boil. Boil gently 10 minutes.
Remove jars and place on a towel and cover with a towel.
The jars should pop and seal.
Refrigerate any jars that do not seal.

Note:
I measure the fruit and juice in a dry measuring cup so I can level it with a knife and get the exact amount. To make it easier when placing and removing the jars from the boiling water, use a "jar lifter"; it is a special tool made specifically for this task.

English Toffee
Maria Smythe

This is so good you will have to hide it. But can you trust yourself?

Cook Time: 15 minutes
Yield: 9X13 pan

Ingredients:
1 cup butter
1 cup sugar
1/4 cup water
8 ounces slivered almonds
1 heaping tablespoon Karo syrup
8 ounces milk chocolate, chopped into small pieces, or chocolate chips
2 ounces slivered almonds processed in a blender until very small for dusting

Directions:
Set aside a 9X13 cookie sheet or baking pan with sides.
Put butter, sugar, water, almonds, and Karo syrup in a 10.5 or 11 inch nonstick skillet.
Heat on high heat stirring constantly.
When it gets thick, keep flipping it. Stirring constantly.
Turn heat down a little so it doesn't burn.
When it is thick and the color of a brown paper bag, dump out on the cookie sheet, spread out. Immediately spread out the chocolate on top of the toffee.
Let the chocolate sit a couple minutes to melt.
When melted spread with a rubber spatula until smooth.
Sprinkle the powdered almonds on top. Refrigerate immediately.
When hardened, lift the corner with a dull knife and break apart.
Store in a sealed container in the refrigerator.

Megan's Toffee
Megan McCollum

Our cousin Megan makes dozens of batches of this toffee and delivers them to everyone she knows at Christmas. Her toffee tins are always received with excitement and hugs! She assures me she can make 8 batches in 2 hours.

Cook Time: 15 minutes
Yield: 1- 9 inch pie plate

Ingredients:
1/2 cup unsalted butter
1/2 cup plus 2 tablespoons sugar
Generous pinch kosher salt
1 bowl with 2 tablespoons water
1/2 cup chopped pecans, divided
1 1/2 Hershey's chocolate bars or 1/2 big dark chocolate bar, chopped

Directions:
Premeasure the sugar and put it in a bowl.
Add the salt to the sugar.
Put 1/4 cup chopped pecans in a Pyrex pie plate.
Unwrap and break up the chocolate, set aside.
In a 10 inch omelet pan on medium heat, melt butter until bubbly, being careful not to burn.
Add 2 tablespoons water, bring to a boil.
Add sugar and salt, all at once.
Stir over medium heat until it gets thick and the color of a brown paper bag.
Pour it on top of the pecans in the pie plate.
Wipe the pan with a paper towel to start the next batch.
Let the toffee sit a couple minutes until still hot, but a little firm, then sprinkle the chocolate on top. When the chocolate has melted, spread it around with a rubber spatula and top with the remainder 1/4 cup of pecans.
Put in a cool place to harden.
Break apart with an old butter knife. It will be very hard.
Store in an airtight container.

Peanut Butter Balls
Irene McKinney

This recipe is one of our family traditions at Christmas. We have a photo of our oldest daughter Karen as an 11- month-old with her hand in the tin!

Yield: 100 balls

Ingredients:
2 1/2 cups butter
3 1/2 pounds confectioners sugar, sifted
2 1/2 pounds smooth peanut butter, I like Skippy
3/4 of 1 square of paraffin wax
16 ounces semi-sweet chocolate chips

Directions:
In a double boiler over simmering heat, melt wax and chips.
In a large bowl mix butter, confectioners sugar and peanut butter with your hands until smooth and all the sugar is mixed in.
Roll into balls, refrigerate.
The dipping goes better with cold peanut butter balls.
Move the balls around on the cookie sheet to loosen them.
Stick toothpicks in a bunch and dip in the melted chocolate.
Place on a parchment-lined cookie sheet to harden. Keep refrigerated.

Notes:
I find if you use an inexpensive peanut butter they are crumbly instead of creamy.

Alternative chocolate-you can buy a premium chocolate and temper it to dip your balls into. This is what I do when I sell them at the Surry Store.

Swedish Nuts

Sherri Hebert

Every Christmas our coworker Sherri would bring in candy tins of these and leave them in the break room. Word spread quickly and they would disappear. If you have any leftover, they are great in a salad. They also make great Christmas gifts. When I called Sheri to ask if I could use this recipe in our cookbook, she said, "Donna, I gave you that recipe 25 times." I laughed and said, "I have it, I just want to share it," and she happily agreed.

Cook Time: 325º 30 minutes
Yield: 1 pound

Ingredients:
2 egg whites
1 cup sugar
1 pinch salt
3/4 teaspoon vanilla
16 ounces pecan halves
1/2 cup butter

Directions:
Preheat oven to 325º.
Melt butter on baking sheet. Don't use the bottom oven rack.
Beat egg whites until soft peaks form.
Add sugar, salt, and vanilla.
Beat until glossy, will not hold a peak.
Fold in nuts. Coat well.
Place on the baking sheet on the melted butter.
Bake at 325º 30 minutes, turn every 10 minutes until all the butter is absorbed.
Cool.
Will store in an airtight container several weeks.

Homemade Granola

Donna Doyen

Cook Time: 250º 45 minutes. Stir every 10 minutes.
Yield: 14 cups

Ingredients:
8 cups old fashioned oats
1 cup sesame seeds
1 cup poppy seeds
1-10 ounce bag sliced almonds
1-8 ounce bag pecans
1 cup dark brown sugar or 1/3 cup honey, 1/3 cup dark brown sugar, and 1/3 cup maple syrup
1/2 cup olive oil or butter
1 cup dried apricots, cut up
1-16 ounce bag craisins

Directions:
Preheat oven to 250º.
Mix dry ingredients (not the fruit). Put in a large baking pan.
Mix together brown sugar, honey, and maple syrup pour over oat mixture, stir.
Bake, stirring every 10 minutes.
Cool completely. Store in airtight containers.
I add fruit when I use it so it doesn't get hard.
Notes:
Great on yogurt. No sugar version-1/2 cup each of honey and maple syrup.

Nut and Seed Bars
Blue Hill Co-Op

When travelling I like to keep baggies of this in my car door. If I get hungry or sleepy, I eat it right out of the bag. In the winter it is hard and in the summer it's gooey.

Ingredients:
4 cups mixed raw nuts: cashews, almonds, pecans, walnuts, peanuts
4 cups seeds (pumpkin, sunflower)
2 cups raisins or craisins
2 cups brown rice syrup

Directions:
In a large pan heat rice syrup until bubbly. Add nuts, seeds, and dried fruit. Mix well. Press onto a cookie sheet with a piece of parchment paper or wax paper sprayed with Pam, press firmly.

Notes: Store in sandwich bags. Keeps well, makes great energy bars!

Acknowledgements

I would like to acknowledge the people who have helped me complete this book. Thank you to our family, friends, and customers who have been so patient over the years waiting for this collection of cherished recipes.

Thank you Phil, my husband, who has put in as many hours as I have editing and formatting on the computer so it could be sent off to the publisher. My appreciation goes out to our daughters: Karen, Katherine, and Elizabeth, who have provided valued suggestions, editing, and technical support.

Thanks to Tracy Thurston for her countless hours photographing the almost endless array of food coming out of our kitchen, as well as her time and dedication editing photos.

Thanks to Teddi-Jann Covell for illustrating our bed and breakfast in such a beautiful style.

Thanks to Linda Greenlaw for her support, encouragement, and forward. Linda's coaching helped me to realize and achieve the full potential of this cookbook.

Thanks to Rackliffe Pottery in Blue Hill, Maine. Margaret and Denny's beautiful handcrafted pottery adds a great backdrop to my creations.

Thanks to Donnie Joseph for final editing and technical expertise.

Thank you Maribeth Salois for the precious watercolor of our home which adorns our dining room wall.

Thank you Antonio Martin for the beautiful photos of Wave Walker at night.

Thank you Sue Michaud for your lovely photos of our home.

I would also like to thank all the friends and family who have shared their most treasured and well-loved recipes.

Lastly, thanks to our customers who were the impetus to write this cookbook. They have been the constant motivation and inspiration that I needed to complete this two-year journey.

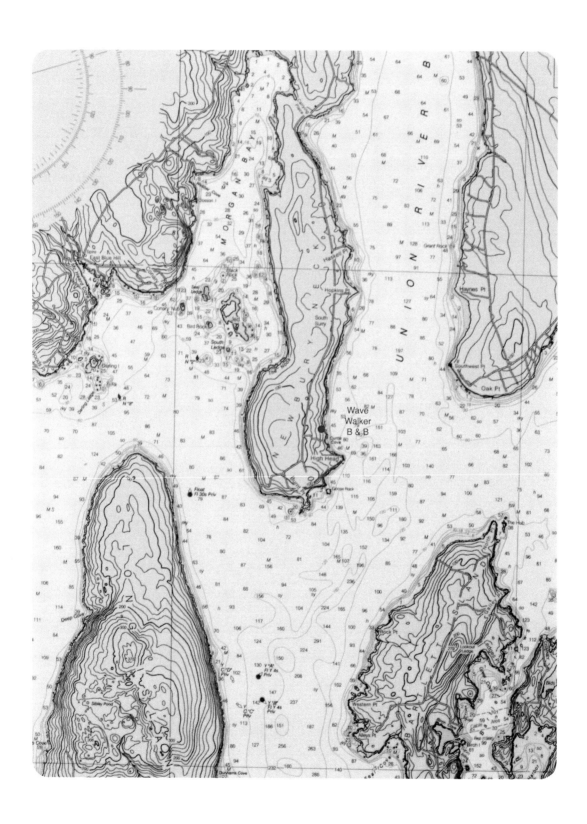

About the Author

Donna and Philip Doyen are the owners and innkeepers at Wave Walker Bed and Breakfast in Surry, ME. They are retired air traffic controllers, who have begun a new adventure on the picturesque Maine coast. Donna has been a life-long home baker and cook, since learning the love of good food and the joys of hospitality at her grandmother's knee. Donna and Phil have three daughters who are no strangers to the kitchen. Donna loves how food brings people together, whether it is a holiday, or just a cup of tea and a muffin with a neighbor. Donna enjoys swapping recipes and stories with her guests, who come from around the world and next door.

Wave Walker Bed and Breakfast was Philip's idea. Phil and his brother inherited 83 acres of pristine oceanfront property on the Blue Hill Peninsula from their mother. Their grandmother, Esther Greenstein Kettell, purchased the farm house and property in 1928 and passed it on to their mother, Elizabeth Doyen. Phil and his brother Malcolm grew up on the property playing in the woods, throwing rocks in the ocean, pulling lobster traps in the bay, and learning to sail right in their backyard. Phil wanted to share the property and love for the Maine coast with others. He knew we had a beautiful location, and he knew Donna would be a wonderful host and chef. So the idea of a B&B was born.

Wave Walker is situated on a 20 acre blueberry field with nearly 1,000 feet of deep water ocean frontage overlooking Acadia National Park. After three years of construction, the four-room bed and breakfast with a nearby guest house opened in 2010. Each year, new and returning guests are pampered with decadent 3-course breakfasts and luxurious accommodations. Wave Walker has won awards of excellence from Yankee Magazine and TripAdvisor.

Recipe index

Baked Goods 13
  Grandma Doyen's Blueberry Muffins 14
  Pumpkin Bread or Muffins 15
  Banana Nut Muffins 16
  Cranberry Orange Muffins 17
  Rhubarb, Orange, and Ginger Muffins 18
  Morning Glory Muffins 19
  Vegan Carrot Cake Muffins 20
  Gluten Free Banana Peanut Butter Muffins 21
  Paleo Pumpkin Muffins 22
  Blueberry Buttermilk Scones 23
  Blueberry Almond Scones with Lemon Curd 24
  Gluten Free Blueberry Coconut Scones 25
  Rhubarb Coffee Cake with Caramel Sauce 26
  Rhubarb Coffeecake 27
  Rhubarb Coffeecake with Streusel & Glaze 28
  Poppy Seed Cake 29
  Cinnamon Streusel Coffeecake 30
  Blueberry Cream Cheese Coffeecake 31
  Apple Pound Cake 32
  Blood Orange Yogurt Bread 33
  Zucchini Bread 34
  Irish Brown Bread 35
  Pecan Sticky Buns Yeast Dough 36
  Blueberry Yeast Rolls 38
Fruit Sensations 41
  Spinach Grape Pineapple Smoothie 42
  Blueberry Smoothie 43
  Kale Apple Lemon Smoothie 44
  Baked Pears 45
  Baked Pears with Fresh Ginger and Honey 46
  Poached Plums 47
  Poached Peaches with Grand Marnier Reduction 48
  Soft Custard 49
  Peach Torte 50
Breakfast Entrées 51
  Lobster Omelet 52
  Crustless Mini Crab Quiche 54
  German Apple Pancake 55

Raspberry Stuffed French Toast 56

Lemon Raspberry French Toast Strata 57

Egg Crêpes 58

Crème Brulee French Toast 59

Breakfast Sausage Strata 60

Aebleskivers 61

Corned Beef Hash 62

Stuffed Portobello Mushroom Delight 63

Zucchini Frittata 64

Apple, Sage, and Fennel Sausage 65

Parmesan Potatoes 66

Appetizers 67

Maine Lobster Stew 68

Easy Crab Dip on Bread 69

Scallops Wrapped in Bacon 70

Caprese Roasted Tomatoes 71

Beef Tenderloin with Horseradish Cream 72

Portobello Mushrooms with Bacon and Tomato 73

Baked Stuffed Mushrooms 74

Arugula and Beet Salad 75

Blueberry Crostinis 76

Black Bean Dip, Fat Free 77

Baked Beans with Ham and Bacon 78

Black Bean Soup 79

Lobsters and More for Dinner 81

New England Lobster Pie 82

Lobster Macaroni and Cheese 83

Scallops with Pumpkin Cream Sauce 84

Lasagna with Meat Sauce 85

Baby Back Ribs 86

Beef Roast 87

Bone in Pork Roast 88

Chicken with Lemon and Rosemary 89

Chicken with Sliced Almonds 90

Chicken Orzo 91

Chicken Piccata 92

Crab potatoes, "Crab Unique" 93

Lobster Potato Salad 94

Roasted Cauliflower 95

Baked Stuffed Loaded Potatoes 96

Desserts 97

Grandma's McKinney's Pie Crust 98

Old Fashioned Rhubarb Pie 99

 139

No Bake Blueberry Pie 100
Strawberry Rhubarb Pie 101
Pumpkin Pie 102
Peanut Butter Pie 103
Blueberry Pie 104
Apple Cranberry Pie 106
Slush Cake 107
Blueberry Cake with Lemon Sauce 108
Rum Cake 109
Blueberry Buckle 110
Lemon Pudding Cakes 111
Carrot Cake 112
Blueberry Slump 113
Chocolate Fudgy Truffle Cheesecake 114
Rhubarb Cheesecake 116
Strawberry Rhubarb Crisp 117
Oatmeal Cookies 118
Chocolate Cake 119
Donna's Pantry Sauces, Jams, and Candy 121
Blueberry Sauce 122
Blueberry Compote 123
Charlotte's Hot Fudge Sauce 124
Rhubarb Sauce 125
Hollandaise Sauce 126
Strawberry Rhubarb Jam 127
English Toffee 128
Megan's Toffee 129
Peanut Butter Balls 130
Swedish Nuts 131
Homemade Granola 132
Nut and Seed Bars 133

Recipe Index Alphabetical

Aebleskivers 61

Apple Cranberry Pie 106

Apple Pound Cake 32

Apple, Sage, and Fennel Sausage 65

Arugula and Beet Salad 75

Baby Back Ribs 86

Baked Beans with Ham and Bacon 78

Baked Pears 45

Baked Pears with Fresh Ginger and Honey 46

Baked Stuffed Loaded Potatoes 96

Baked Stuffed Mushrooms 74

Banana Nut Muffins 16

Beef Roast 87

Beef Tenderloin with Horseradish Cream 72

Black Bean Dip, Fat Free 77

Black Bean Soup 79

Blood Orange Yogurt Bread 33

Blueberry Almond Scones with Lemon Curd 24

Blueberry Buckle 110

Blueberry Buttermilk Scones 23

Blueberry Cake with Lemon Sauce 108

Blueberry Compote 123

Blueberry Cream Cheese Coffeecake 31

Blueberry Crostinis 76

Blueberry Pie 104

Blueberry Sauce 122

Blueberry Slump 113

Blueberry Smoothie 43

Blueberry Yeast Rolls 38

Bone in Pork Roast 88

Breakfast Sausage Strata 60

Caprese Roasted Tomatoes 71

Carrot Cake 112

Charlotte's Hot Fudge Sauce 124

Chicken Orzo 91

Chicken Piccata 92

Chicken with Lemon and Rosemary 89

Chicken with Sliced Almonds 90

Chocolate Cake 119

Chocolate Fudgy Truffle Cheesecake 114

Cinnamon Streusel Coffeecake..30

Corned Beef Hash 62

Crab potatoes, "Crab Unique" 93

Cranberry Orange Muffins...17

Crème Brulee French Toast..59

Crustless Mini Crab Quiche...54

Easy Crab Dip on Bread 69

Egg Crêpes..58

Eggs Benedict Sauce..126

English Toffee..128

German Apple Pancake 55

Gluten Free Banana Peanut Butter Muffins 21

Gluten Free Blueberry Coconut Scones..25

Grandma Doyen's Blueberry Muffins..14

Grandma's McKinney's Pie Crust 98

Hollandaise Sauce 126

Homemade Granola...132

Irish Brown Bread...35

Kale Apple Lemon Smoothie 44

Lasagna with Meat Sauce 85

Lemon Pudding Cakes...111

Lemon Raspberry French Toast Strata 57

Lobster Macaroni and Cheese..83

Lobster Omelet 52

Lobster Potato Salad...94

Maine Lobster Stew 68

Megan's Toffee 129

Morning Glory Muffins 19

New England Lobster Pie 82

No Bake Blueberry Pie..100

Nut and Seed Bars 133

Oatmeal Cookies 118

Old Fashioned Rhubarb Pie 99

Paleo Pumpkin Muffins 22

Parmesan Potatoes...66

Peach Torte 50

Peanut Butter Balls 130

Peanut Butter Pie 103

Pecan Sticky Buns Yeast Dough...36

Poached Peaches with Grand Marnier Reduction 48

Poached Plums..47

Poppy Seed Cake..29

Portobello Mushrooms with Bacon and Tomato 73

Pumpkin Bread or Muffins 15

Pumpkin Pie 102

Raspberry Stuffed French Toast 56

Rhubarb Cheesecake 116

Rhubarb Coffee Cake with Caramel Sauce 26

Rhubarb Coffeecake 27

Rhubarb Coffeecake with Streusel & Glaze 28

Rhubarb Sauce 125

Rhubarb, Orange, and Ginger Muffins 18

Roasted Cauliflower 95

Rum Cake 109

Scallops with Pumpkin Cream Sauce 84

Scallops Wrapped in Bacon 70

Slush Cake 107

Soft Custard 49

Spinach Grape Pineapple Smoothie 42

Strawberry Rhubarb Crisp 117

Strawberry Rhubarb Jam 127

Strawberry Rhubarb Pie 101

Stuffed Portobello Mushroom Delight 63

Swedish Nuts 131

Vegan Carrot Cake Muffins 20

Zucchini Bread 34

Zucchini Frittata 64

Key Word Index Alphabetical

Abeleskeiver 61

Almond 20, 21, 22, 24, 25, 27, 29, 43, 90, 128, 132, 133

Ann Shafer 110

Apple 19, 20, 131, 32, 34, 42, 44, 55, 65, 102, 106

Arugula 75

Avis Black 30, 99

Banana 61, 21, 42, 43, 49, 61

Baumgarten, John 79

Bean 48, 77, 78, 79

Beardsley, Betty 29

Beef 62, 67, 72, 87

Betty Beardsley 29

Betty Mathien 78

Black, Avis 30, 99

Blue Hill Co-Op 133

Blueberry 14, 23, 24, 25, 31, 38, 43, 56, 58, 76, 100, 104, 108, 110, 113, 122, 123

Bonnie Torrey 69

Bread 15, 21, 29, 30, 32, 33, 34, 35, 56, 57, 59, 60, 67, 69, 72, 74, 76, 84, 85

Cake 20, 21, 25, 26, 27, 28, 29, 30, 31, 32, 33, 54, 55, 61, 96, 107, 109, 109, 111, 112, 114, 115, 116, 119, 122, 125

Caron, Karen 112

Carrot 19, 20, 79, 112

Cauliflower 95

Charlotte McCollum 90, 109, 124

Cheesecake 114, 115, 116, 125

Chicken 79, 89, 90, 91, 92

Chocolate 43, 62, 103, 107, 114, 115, 119, 124, 128, 129, 230

Claire Strong 15

Coconut 19, 21, 22, 25, 42

Coffee 21, 26, 27, 28, 30, 31, 124

Compote 111, 123

Cookie 21, 114, 118

Crab 54, 67, 69, 98

Cranberry 16, 17, 106

Cream cheese 31, 50, 56, 70, 103, 107, 112, 113, 114, 115, 116

Crepes 58, 122, 125

Crisp 117

Curd 14, 23, 24, 113, 122

Dip 67, 69, 77

Donna Doyen 16, 18, 19, 23, 24, 32, 38, 42, 43, 44, 46, 48, 52, 54, 56, 58, 60, 63, 68, 69, 70, 73, 74, 85, 86, 94, 101, 103, 104,

Donna Doyen Continued 106, 114, 117, 127, 132

Donna Polinski 50

Dough 36, 98

Doyen, Elizabeth 14, 108, 122

Fennel 65

Fletcher, Sherry 72, 77, 95

Free 16, 17, 21, 25, 55, 74, 79

French toast 56, 57, 59

Frittata 64

Ginger 18, 46, 102

Gluten 17, 21, 25, 55, 73, 74, 79

Grape 42, 44

Hash 62

Hebert, Sherri 131

Helen Martin Orth 124

Hollandaise 126

Honey 22, 46, 132

Irene McKinney 34, 49, 98, 102, 130

Irish 35

Jam 56, 58, 62, 121, 127

Janericco, Terence 57, 65, 83, 122

Jean Messex 69

John Baumgarten 79

Johnson, Richard 47

Kale 41, 42, 44

Karen Caron 112

Kelly Sawyer 62

Laurie Rokakis 20

Lemon 14, 23, 24, 31, 34, 38, 39, 44, 47, 57, 59, 75, 77, 89, 92, 94, 95, 104, 105, 108, 111, 113, 122, 123, 125, 126

Lisa Mitchell 93

Lobster 52, 53, 68, 81, 82, 83, 94

Macaroni 83

Maria Messier 84, 113, 116

Maria Smythe 128

Markel's Bakehouse 62

Marnier 48, 59

Martin, Orth Helen 24

Mathien, Betty 78

McCollum, Charlotte 90, 109, 124

McCollum, Megan 57,71, 89, 96, 129

McKinney, Irene 34, 49, 98, 102, 130

Megan, McCollum 57, 71, 89, 96, 129

Messex, Jean 69

Messier, Maria 84, 113, 116

Mitchell, Lisa 93

Muffin 14, 15, 16, 17, 18, 19, 20, 21, 22

Mushroom 63, 65, 67, 73, 74, 85

Omelet 9, 52, 53, 129

Orange 17, 18, 29, 33, 42, 44, 48, 59, 62, 75

Orzo 91

Ouellette, Robin 100

Paleo 22

Pancake 55, 61, 122, 125

Peach 48, 50

Peanut 21, 43, 61, 103, 130

Peanut butter 21, 43, 61, 103, 130

Pear 45, 46, 48

Pecan 19, 22, 36, 37, 50, 76, 109, 117, 118, 124, 129, 131, 132, 133

Pie 22, 82, 98, 99, 100, 101, 102, 103, 104, 105, 106

Plum 47, 48

Poached 47, 48, 62

Polinski, Donna 50

Portobello 63, 67, 73

Pumpkin 15, 22, 32, 84, 102

Quiche 54

Raspberry 56, 57, 125

Rhubarb 18, 26, 27, 28, 99, 101, 104, 105, 116, 117, 125, 127

Richard Johnson 47

Robin Ouellette 100

Rokakis, Laurie 20

Salad 75, 94

Sauce 26, 36, 37, 59, 84, 85, 86, 92, 108, 121, 122, 123, 124, 125, 126

Sausage 60, 61, 65, 74, 79, 85

Sawyer, Kelly 62

Scones 23, 24, 25

Shafer, Ann 110

Sherri Hebert 131

Sherry Fletcher 72, 77, 95

Slump 113

Smoothie 20, 42, 43, 44

Smythe, Maria 128

Soup 79

Spinach 41, 42, 44, 63, 65, 73

Stew 68

Strata 57, 70

Strawberry 101, 117, 127

Streusel 28, 30

Strong, Claire 15

Terence Janericco 57, 65, 83, 122

Thurston, Tracy 2, 75, 135

Toffee 128, 129

Tomato 63, 67, 71, 73, 85, 91, 92

Torrey, Bonnie 69

Tort 50

Tracy Thurston 2, 75, 135

Tropical 52

Vegan 20

Vegetarian 20

Yeast 21, 36, 37, 38, 39

Yogurt 18, 24, 33, 41, 42, 43, 45, 46, 47, 48, 96, 132

Zucchini 20, 34, 64